BECOMING A MUSICIAN

BECOMING A MUSICIAN

GEORGE NORWOOD HUMPHREY

To order additional copies of this book, contact:
Xlibris Corporation
1-888-795-4274
www.Xlibris.com
Orders@Xlibris.com
34064

CONTENTS

FOREWORD

My father wrote this autobiography of his life in music in 1977 and 1978 after retiring from the Boston Symphony in the spring of 1977. He had had forty-three seasons with the Symphony, joining it in the fall of 1934. After he had finished the autobiography, he made attempts to have it published, discussing the possibility with his friend, the journalist and historian, William L. Shirer. His efforts were unsuccessful, however, and he subsequently turned the manuscript over to me. I read and enjoyed it, but did nothing with it because he had already tried.

Recently, though, I thought that at least it should be in the symphony archives, and over a period of two to three months, I retyped it using a word processor so that it could be easily reproduced. At the same time, I did some preliminary editing, mostly correcting the few typographical errors (he was an expert typist, after all). I also thought that there might be a few people within the family and outside who would be interested in reading it.

My father was born on August 25, 1904, in Bellaire, Ohio, where he grew up and attended the Bellaire public schools, graduating from Bellaire High School. He was the son of George Latham Humphrey, who was an engineer on the Pennsylvania Railroad, then a position of some prestige, much like a senior airline pilot today. His mother was Mabel Long Humphrey, a demonstrative and caring woman. He had two younger brothers: one who died in childbirth, and the other, Robert.

After graduating from high school, my father went to work as a clerk in the Pennsylvania Railroad, where he met my mother, Mildred Weber, who is from Mingo Junction, Ohio, and was born in 1904, less than a month later than my father. He and my mother were married in 1929, a few months after his graduation from the New England Conservatory. I was born in 1931, my brother John in 1932, and my brother Eric in 1938. When my mother and father eventually settled in Greater Boston, they first lived in Medford, then in Somerville, and finally in 1938 in Arlington, where he lived the rest of his life.

Besides the pursuits mentioned in his book, my father also made several violas, one of which won a prize in an international competition. He had several pupils. He also sailed a great deal in the summer, mostly at Tanglewood. He played golf and once told me he thought he might have been good enough to go on the pro tour. He was not. For several summers in the 1940s and 1950s, he chose not to go to Tanglewood (for a time, he was permitted to do that) and was a member of an excellent small orchestral group that was resident in the summers at the Lake Placid Club in Lake Placid, New York. Most of its members were from the Eastman School in Rochester, New York. During the 1960s, my father was a member of a team at the Massachusetts Institute of Technology involved in a study of acoustics.

His true, lifelong love was chamber music, and for many years, he and the Tanglewood Quartet each year gave a concert at the Harvard Musical Association, where he was a longtime member, and at the Harvard Club. He also regularly gathered other musicians together in Tanglewood and Lake Placid and at our house and other homes for informal chamber music sessions.

After his retirement from the Symphony, he finished his autobiography and then suffered a decline in his health, which involved several cranial operations. He died on April 23, 1980. My mother celebrated her 102nd birthday on September 12, 2006, and is living at Norumbega Point in Weston, Massachusetts, still quite vigorous.

I wish to thank Bill and Betsy Moyer for their review of the manuscript and their many valuable suggestions. Before his retirement, Bill was the personnel director of the orchestra and knew my father personally, and he endorsed many of my father's reminiscences. Bridget Carr, the archivist of the Symphony, has generously provided many of the photographs shown herein. Additionally, my wife Diana undertook the job of the final edit of the material, and her contribution was truly valuable.

January 2007

George Lee Humphrey

CHAPTER 1

The Early Years

I had never heard a symphony orchestra before that night in 1923 when I found myself listening to the New York Philharmonic in Wheeling, West Virginia. Willem Mengelberg conducted, I remember, though it could have been anyone else as far as I was concerned. The program has long been forgotten, but later familiarity with the work of Mengelberg, learned through others, assures me that it was no doubt Teutonic and on the heavy side.

One moment does come back to me when I heard one lady ask another, "What is the difference between a symphony and a philharmonic orchestra?" Her friend answered, "A symphony orchestra plays only symphonies; a philharmonic orchestra can play anything it wishes!" This explanation sufficed for me too at the time.

I couldn't have been familiar with the work of the Philharmonic or any other orchestra, for such a visit was rare indeed. Recordings of symphonic groups were not then easily available unless under special order, and I was not one who would have had the musical education as a spur to seek them out. I was attending this concert as a guest of my friend, Edwin Heatherington, who, in my little town of Bellaire, Ohio, only four miles away from Wheeling, had a considerable knowledge of the world's better music and generously tried to interest others in the world of sound. Edwin worked as a bookkeeper in one of our local industrial concerns during the day, but his evenings were given over to his other loves, music and literature. He owned one of the only Welte-Mignon grand pianos in town and a large store of rolls to play through it.

Edwin and I, through our memberships in the local Knights of Pythias lodge, had become friends, and he must have recognized in me something of which I was still unaware. I was nineteen at the time with no musical training behind me. I had tried to play the violin, it is true, but had not succeeded to even a small extent. My wish, could it have been granted, would have been to play like Fritz Kreisler. At the moment I would not have been tempted to learn to play an instrument for a career in an orchestra, even one such as this. I had ears only for the tones of the solo violin as played by Kreisler, tones that found their way into my very soul.

My parents came from simple, hardworking ancestry that bestowed upon me a combination of Scotch, Irish, Welsh, and German blood. On my father's side, our American family began in 1634, the first of our name, John Humphrey, having been a colonial governor of the area now known as Swampscott, Massachusetts. My mother's family had been in America for more than several generations, but its earlier history has eluded me. My father, the only member of his family to desert the family farm in Smyrna, Ohio, had become a railroad engineer and eventually established a home in this little town of Bellaire, where my brother and I grew up. Railroading, coal mining, steel production, and glassmaking provided employment for practically all its residents.

There was little time for other considerations. A childhood spent in those surroundings would hardly inspire one to look toward the arts for his life's work. The fascination with the scenes around one would be enough to keep most of my childhood friends close to their beginnings.

To this day I can feel the lure of the railroad, the heady smell of soft coal smoke mixed with steam, the *chuff chuff* of the huge locomotives as they started their hundred-car trains. Even the sight of the exhaust from the blast furnaces as they threw their glare high into the night cannot be forgotten, and the combination of those sights and smells was reason enough for a young person fascinated by what went on about him to remain in the area.

Yet I broke away. In the normal order of things, with still one year of high school before me, I accepted a job as crew clerk with the Pennsylvania Railroad, my father's employer. That I had to work the night shift, 11:00 p.m. to 7:00 a.m., did not deter me, though I had to attend school from 9:00 a.m. to 4:00 p.m. It was part of an exciting life!

My final year of school went by in a dreamlike trance. Awake at night, half-asleep during my class-filled days, I saw the end of my school days approach through half-closed lids. I actually fell asleep during the baccalaureate address delivered to our class!

Sometime during those early years, I had heard my father draw tones from a fiddle, one borrowed from a friend. He had managed to keep a small amount of facility on his favorite instrument, which at one time he had played for barn dances. Eventually, he had been able to buy a secondhand outfit from a friendly dealer. For violin, bow, and case, he paid $2!

I used to ask him to show me how those sounds were gotten, but he was unable to transmit his own knowledge. I learned from him by keeping my eyes on his every movement. It was probably in my first year of high school that I had the temerity to try to play with the high school orchestra. At least I filled in a place when the orchestra picture was taken. Then my father's fiddle was put back in its case for a long rest. I forgot its existence.

In truth, I was far more interested in the study of typing. I had been surprised at my interest in the subject, probably because I had found my fingers faster than my fellow students as I took the subject in my junior year. Perhaps they were not as interested as I. With after-school practice, my own etudes or finger exercises, I had raised my typing speed to 145 words per minute, equal to the record set by George Hossfelt, world-champion professional typist. After a demonstration given in our assembly room by Albert Tangora, champion amateur typist of the world, when he attained a speed of 210 words per minute using a sentence designed only for such a purpose, I heeded my typing instructor's encouragement and was able, within a few days, to attain a speed of 232 words per minute on the same sentence. In that one-minute race with time, I was striking 13 1/2 strokes per second. A life as a speed typist or court stenographer seemed possible, so I thought strongly of enrolling myself in the Bliss Business School of Columbus, Ohio.

In those years of low wages, long work shifts, the amount of $140 per month, my salary with the railroad, seemed like a high amount. And I was still in school! I saw no reason why I should not now buy my mother something she had often spoken of—a Victrola. It came from me as a Christmas gift to her with its added gift from the dealer of ten records: nine of Paul Whiteman's Orchestra, one of Fritz Kreisler, the violinist.

Over and over I played those Whiteman records, the Kreisler disc having been put aside as being beyond my comprehension. It took weeks of assaulting my ears with foxtrot rhythms before I was ready to hear the Kreisler record, if for nothing else, to escape the constant beat of the dance music. Even so, I had to hear the Caprice Viennois more than several times before I began to sense that I had neglected a treasure trove of beauties: one of the music itself, the other the richness of sound produced by this magician of the violin.

Here were the moments when I began to sense the beauty of a world far removed from that which I knew, to feel the pull of urgings I could not reduce to words, to experience being carried from the spot I occupied to far places by the power and beauty of the music being played.

Slowly, then eagerly, I began to build up a record library of Kreisler's playing. As my idolatry for him grew, I regarded as heretics those who would speak the names of Elman or Heifetz. Driven by this idolatry, my next step was to purchase an instrument with which to emulate my god and then to purchase the music from which these inspired sounds came. But in vain! I could not draw those sounds from my $15 violin nor could I even read the music.

I approached a local violin teacher and learned from him that what I hoped to do was impossible, for I was more than nineteen years old. A $2 lesson fee must have looked as good to him as it looked large to me, so we put aside all doubts and made a beginning. Weekly lessons and daily practice became my habits, for I had now graduated from high school with only the railroad to call me away from my violin.

In the midst of these pleasures, my teacher announced that he had nothing more to teach me—after only six months! He advised me to seek specialized instruction, possibly from a conservatory of music. With no guide but myself, I wrote to the Bureau of Information in Washington for information on the subject and learned that the New England Conservatory of Music in Boston was the leading music school of the day. With that, my way became clear. Toward the day when I should enroll myself at the Conservatory, I began saving a good portion of my salary. Eventually I asked for a leave of absence from the railroad and was refused, since it was not a leave which would benefit the railroad. Having seen my bank balance reach the total of $1,000, I simply resigned my position, by that time a good one in the master mechanic's office. My bridges were burned by my ambition to become a musician, and I set out for Boston.

In choosing a teacher from the imposing list in the Conservatory's catalogue, I thought along the line so common to our people at the time. The more foreign or strange sounding the name, the more the teacher must know about music and its performance. I chose the first name on the list, unpronounceable to me, and obviously the head of the violin department.

Fortunately, as it later turned out, his class was full. I was forced to allow my name to be entered in the class of an unknown—to me—Eugene Gruenberg. I say fortunately, for I was soon to discover that my first choice, though a brilliant player in a day long gone, was unable to impart his qualities to others, so his teaching abilities were hardly better than mediocre. My "second choice," on the other hand, was more noted for his teaching skill than he had ever been for his playing, and his pupils were living evidence of that skill. He had been a classmate of Fritz Kreisler, Felix Winternitz, and Franz Kneisel, names held high in Boston's musical circles.

Through the years, auditions have brought out the worst in me. My examiners became my inquisitors, waiting to pounce on every slight inaccuracy. The more I have learned, the more conscious I have become of my own failings. I tighten during auditions beyond any possibility of delivering even my average performance.

But when I appeared for my audition with Gruenberg, I knew so little that I was not yet bound by later shackles of knowledge. I fiddled my way through the difficulties of Viotti's Twenty-third Concerto, over which I had slaved for months before my arrival in Boston. As I turned to Gruenberg for the words of commendation I hoped to hear, I heard him say, "My poy, everything you have learned has been wrong. You must forget the habits you have taken on and begin again." As my house of cards collapsed, he went on, "If you are able to work very hard, you may be able to become a capable player even at your age, and I will try to help you."

He told me that he had begun later than many and knew that a violinist can improve his technique until he becomes forty, an age far in my future, for he had seen it to be so in his own case. I had had little encouragement in my own home, my parents having come to the conclusion, I was later to learn, that I could only be convinced of the impossibility of my task by making the attempt—and failing. These gentle words of Gruenberg were to be my strength.

That first year at the Conservatory passed in a fever of work. All my life I had known people who had worked in twelve-hour shifts and considered it a normal working day. I had worked an eight-hour shift and still had several hours to practice my violin. So I put myself to a regimen of ten hours' daily practice—think of it! I kept a chart on my wall and marked each day as it passed with inward apologies if I failed to make the ten-hour quota.

That first year saw me lose thirty pounds. And I reached the end of my financial resources. In my naiveté and zeal, I had failed to investigate any scholarship that might have been available to me for further study. I hadn't known that application for such must be made before the end of the school year. With my last violin lesson, I said my good-byes, packed my belongings, and set out for Ohio, broke but still ambitious!

I had accomplished enough during that first year for Gruenberg to recommend my studying not only the Bach A Minor Concerto but the Mendelssohn and Wieniawski D Minor as well. I knew he thought me talented, and I had proved that I could work hard.

I worked that summer in the Carnegie Steel Works, wheeling coke dust. Large wheelbarrows, heavy dust, and a long twelve-hour shift with little rest brought my hands to a condition that made it painful to open them at the end of my workday. I couldn't have played even the simplest parts of the works I had brought home to learn.

In September, I counted my savings and found a total of only $200. With this I was supposed to see myself through another year of hard work and study!

My ambition overshadowed my ignorance, and faith drove me on. With a pass provided for me by my father, through his employment with the railroad, I once again set out for the mecca of music, Boston.

I frankly explained my situation to Gruenberg and told him I would get a job and take what lessons I could from time to time. He frowned on that idea and suggested instead that he give me lessons free of charge, only on condition that I not get a job. He felt I had no time to waste. I was compelled to write my father and explain the situation, with the result that he promised to send me $12 per week for living expenses. The two most important demands being satisfied, I set to work once more.

Almost at the beginning of that school year, it was announced that a violist—a former graduate of the Paris Conservatoire and present member of the Boston Symphony—was being added to the faculty. Volunteers were called for to fill his first class of four. Gruenberg had already suggested my playing viola in the orchestra so that I might gain finger strength, reading ability, and orchestral practice. With his blessing, I answered the call that seemed tailored for me. Now I had to answer to two masters.

Inevitably, there was a clash of ideas when I came to study the same piece on both instruments at the same time. There were anxious moments for me at one critical time when I tried to answer my German teacher's question of "how could a Frenchman possibly know anything about the Bach violin sonatas?"

About midway through that term, Gruenberg was rushed to the hospital, where drastic emergency surgery was performed on him. In time, he came home to his apartment to convalesce. He sent for me on a Sunday, and I sat and talked with him as he ate his first postoperative meal. The next morning he was dead, and I had lost a man who had meant more to me than any other up to that moment.

Circumstances thus forced me to become a violist. I was not too unhappy about it, for I had learned that I preferred the deeper beauty of the instrument. My hands seemed to find a greater comfort in its longer reaches, and even my thinking was conditioned toward it because of growing love for the chamber music I had been drawn into. Chamber music was to be the compelling reason for my remaining with music from that time on.

I can look back on four years at the Conservatory that were filled with hard, drudging work. But I acquired a technique on the instrument, a knowledge of chamber music, and a small repertoire of viola works I could perform if opportunity beckoned. For technique's sake, I had invaded the violin repertoire, daring its challenges on the larger instrument. I could have performed certain representative works in public, but it was an unlikely possibility since it would have meant transposing all orchestra or piano parts to fit the key changes almost mandatory in cases of the kind.

The viola was not regarded as a solo instrument. A career along that difficult road need not be my concern. I had, though, to choose between a career as a quartet violist and that of an orchestral player, possibly as leader of a viola section. My inner choice was for the quartet, but it was easier to think about than to accomplish.

The immediate necessity to make a living if I wished to provide for a family and live something of a normal life forced me to set the quartet idea aside, temporarily at least. An orchestra position had to be sought and gained to take care of the debts already incurred, and I looked forward to my own wedding the following October if I was lucky enough to find a position within the profession.

A former classmate had preceded me into symphonic work by a year and was already on tour with the Minneapolis Symphony. At his insistence, I made a special trip to Pittsburgh to meet the orchestra as it stopped there. With his help, I got to play for the conductor Henry Verbrugghen, and within two weeks, I received a contract for the next season. I had not yet graduated from the Conservatory, and I had been at the study of a stringed instrument less than four serious years!

As a final good-bye to the Conservatory, I performed the Handel Concerto with its orchestra during my graduation ceremonies. I was still short of twenty-five years old with the musical world before me. All seemed good.

Though I had performed occasionally with Boston Symphony players on outside jobs during my last two years at the Conservatory, I had yet to learn what it meant to be a full-fledged member of a completely professional group. My experience in the Conservatory orchestra was gained sitting among friends, fellow pupils, or teachers, few of whom criticized others. Now I sat among strangers, discovering for the first time that there were fine players who had never been to Boston. Where had they gained their techniques? Were there other schools of the quality of the Conservatory? Evidently so.

As we swung into the "Euryanthe Overture" that first rehearsal, I found myself left behind in that first brilliant orchestral sweep. I bungled my way back and caught up with my section, though I knew immediately that if I were to be singled out and heard, I would be dismissed at once. I felt hopelessly inadequate. Always before, I had been given time to learn a difficult work, but now I should be required to perform it with a minimum of rehearsal as though I had played it all my life. I felt that the conductor, Verbrugghen, thought me capable. After all, hadn't he responded to my playing in Pittsburgh by playing immediately *for me*? I felt warmly drawn to him. He had been a prodigy pupil of Eugen Ysaye and kept up his playing in addition to his duties as a conductor. As the season progressed, I was to play quartets with him frequently. In that repertoire, I felt much more secure.

I spent that winter in Minneapolis in diligent efforts to learn those works of the repertoire that came before us. Don Juan, Wagner excerpts, Respighi's tone poems, etc.—every one new to me, got my complete attention until I felt that I could hold my own with my colleagues, at least for the moment. Such earnestness had to find its reward, and I suppose I deserved what I reaped.

Several weeks after the season began, I learned that we were to resume an annual radio series for WCCO, the largest local radio station, the first broadcast to be several weeks hence. In a very friendly manner, one of my violist colleagues cautioned me that Verbrugghen was very fussy about the radio theme, "The Ride of the Valkyries." He warned that each year some poor soul was singled out to play, alone, the passagework abounding in the "Ride." If it did not go well, this normally mild-mannered little man flew into an ungovernable rage. I had never seen the piece before but knew at my first glance at it that I was already finished if the notes were expected of me.

The next three weeks saw me using the passages as etudes, working them up a bit faster each day, always with metronome, until I had reached what I thought was a respectable speed. If the conductor held that tempo, I was safe. At the first rehearsal of the radio program, I could hardly hold my bow in my anxiety. As we began the "Ride," I kept waiting for the conductor's eye to turn to me and ask me to play alone. But he looked benignly at us and seemed unconcerned about those fantastically difficult passages I had slaved to learn. Then it was that I saw smirking glances directed toward me and knew that I had been had. I took the joke as it was intended—as a kind of initiation of a greenhorn! But I knew I had done something none of them had—I had played almost all the notes Wagner had written. I can't say I have always done as well since.

It was only shortly after I arrived in Minneapolis that two events of more than minor importance occurred. The first, of major importance to me, was the visit of the Boston Symphony Orchestra to Minneapolis. It dedicated the new Northrop Auditorium of the University of Minnesota that night of October 29, 1929, and, in the doing, swept the audience off its feet. This listener found himself, for the first time, conscious of the power of an orchestra to sway its listeners, of a conductor, Serge Koussevitzky, to carry an audience with him in his quest for perfection and beauty.

Though I had spent four years in Boston, the very home of this peerless organization, I had had no money to spend for listening to it, and my only acquaintance with it was through my teacher, Georges Fourel, or through fellow musicians who had been Conservatory students and occasionally wandered through its corridors. I would have begrudged the time taken from my ceaseless activity of forming daily quartet sessions or from my own viola practice.

The second, of minor importance to me at the time but of major importance to our country and to great areas of the outside world, was the stock market crash that brought on our Great Depression. Both events chose that October 29 for their happening. I remember quite vividly the lines of Boston Symphony players that formed by each telephone booth immediately after that tremendous concert, and I recall my astonishment, perhaps disappointment, that men who could produce such otherworldly sounds from their instruments could still be earthbound enough to engage in market speculation. With these moments, a new era was beginning.

The Minneapolis Symphony's winter schedule took us through a considerable portion of the South and into Cuba, and I got my first taste of the wandering musician's life. I found myself fascinated by the many new places I saw, and to this day I feel that some of the most interesting moments I have spent in symphonic life have come from my travels with an orchestra.

As the spring approached, and with it the end of my first symphony season, it was noised about that raises already promised for the next season were being cancelled. I had been one of those who were to benefit from those raises—in my case from $50 per week to $60—and the idea did not sit too well with me. I had learned that though I lacked experience in orchestra playing and repertoire, I could handle my viola as well as my new colleagues, perhaps even better than some, and the weeks had increased my knowledge and confidence. More than the broken promise, I thought about the season of twenty-six weeks with a corresponding twenty-six weeks of idleness until another season should begin. Staying with the orchestra meant a delay to the move I should eventually have to make if I expected to have a profitable career in music. I had been forced to turn away small engagements during my last year or so at the Conservatory, and I felt that if I were free to accept that sort of engagement back in the city of the cod, I should be as well-off there as I was in Minneapolis. I would no longer be a student at the conservatory with its confining schedule, and I was now a married man who had to look toward the future. A decision was not hard to make.

But it was with regret that I turned away from Minneapolis, the city of my first opportunity. I had grown to love its climate, the beauty of its lake areas, its heavily Scandinavian population. I vowed I would return with every opportunity.

The old 1921 Model T Ford, which had cost me $35 and had been my faithful companion during those six months, gave its last gasp just two days before I was to leave for the East. I salvaged $15 from the wreck by trading it toward a new Model A, the latest thing, but I couldn't raise its full price of $607, so had to take on a debt of $200 to own this elegant new vehicle!

But Boston wasn't the same! Gloom hung over the city—a rash of bankruptcies and suicides had followed the market crash. Music, that luxury item, had been almost the first thing to feel the effect of the business collapse, and the small engagements that had been were no more. Radio stations had cut their staffs to the bone, and those who had felt so secure in their staff orchestra or theater positions were now walking the streets, seeking any opportunity to earn a few dollars within the only profession most of them knew. Some of my old friends, still working, viewed me with suspicion if I even came near their place of employment. And yet where might I have gone? Minneapolis would have given me nothing in those weeks, certainly. I was ready to grasp at any straw.

In my years at the Conservatory, I had heard much talk of the Curtis Institute in Philadelphia and the opportunities to be found there for one with talent. Why, students were even paid to attend! I decided to look into the situation for I was certainly getting nowhere as things stood. Wasting no time, for we had been in

Boston thirty days, we loaded ourselves into our car and headed south. I dropped Mildred at her sister's in New Rochelle and continued on alone.

I braved Curtis Institute one day in late May of that year and learned that Louis Bailly's class had its quota of fourteen. I was told that the age limit for viola students was twenty-three, so I seemed barred on two counts. Still, I explained, I had come many miles to play an audition for him and would appreciate it if I could at least be heard. Within a short time, I found myself playing before this violist of Flonzaley Quartet fame. To my surprise and delight, he agreed to add me to his class. I could start with the class in September. I had the courage and good sense to ask if he intended changing my style of playing, and he replied that he liked what I did and the manner in which I went about it. That was enough. I floated on a cloud back to New Rochelle, rejoined Mildred, and shortly we set out for home in Ohio once more.

Curtis was a much different kind of music school. Here, each student was a child prodigy, or had been. I should estimate that most of my fellow students were in the seventeen- to twenty-year-old group, though some were younger, and in at least two exceptional cases, but thirteen. At twenty-six, I felt rather out of things, for I had not been a prodigy, and I was older than any with whom I made music.

I was to discover that the amounts paid to students varied in size. Each student seemed to have his own level of payment, set by the higher powers through their own system of evaluation. A young coal miner from Italy was being paid not only for himself but for his family which had accompanied him to our country.

For me, there could be nothing. I was told that as I was an extra student in Bailly's class, I could not be considered a true member of the student body, thus no payment. I was reminded that I was overage for the school, thus no payment. And to top it off, since I had already been a professional player in the musical world, I merited no payment. It needed no great brain to understand that with no income whatsoever, it would be impossible for me to put my best efforts into the practice I felt I must have, to get the most the Institute had to offer.

Mildred came to the rescue! She found a job that would pay her $16 per week; and with that amount assured, we set up housekeeping, and I began once more.

But it couldn't go on indefinitely. I was not happy with the state of affairs. We had barely enough to eat, the simplest of furniture, not an extra cent in case of emergency. To top it off, I was finding things at Curtis different than I had expected them to be. Almost with my first lesson, Bailly had begun to change my entire manner of playing.

I was forced to play a viola of a certain size with a most peculiar chin rest that cut me terribly as I tried to practice the odd things I was given to do. I must hold a book under my right arm as I bowed, I must give up any flexibility of my bowing fingers, straighten out my right thumb as I held the bow—all because *he* did it that way. In only a few weeks, I found it impossible to play the piece I had played for my audition.

To my question of how long it would be before I learned to play his way, I got the answer of "two years"—and then I would have come a circle to begin again where I had already been! One had only to look at us as we stood together to realize that neither of us could have played with the same rules as governed the other. I was six feet tall, nearly two hundred pounds of bone and muscle, while he was possibly five feet four, nearly equal my weight but of different content. Padded as he was, he could place the instrument almost anywhere he might desire, and it would sink in and stay. I had to find the right place! Yet he had complimented me on my quartet playing, a field in which he had been preeminent. Eventually, I asked to be allowed to give up viola lessons and concentrate on quartet classes instead and was met with an answer so wrathful that I could feel my anger rising and a decision beginning to work within me.

So it was only a matter of time. I held out as long as I could, and when seven months had elapsed, I simply informed the dean that I was through, let the stores reclaim the furniture I had tried to buy on the installment plan, hocked my watch to pay our way back to Ohio, and our little Ford took us sadly back to where we seemed to belong. I had become sure that music was not to be my career.

In a heated moment between Bailly and myself when I protested that I could never hope to play the viola in his manner since we were so physically unlike, he had cried out, "Don't tell me how to play the viola. I am the greatest viola player in the world!" I was unable to hold my tongue and had answered, "If you were the greatest violist, you would not need to tell anyone!" This brought the reply, "You have no talent. Go back to selling lumber!" Though I had never sold lumber, his meaning was clear enough, and this from the very same lips that had only several months before exclaimed over my talent.

Still, my morale was very low, and I was almost ready to follow his suggestion. Perhaps music was not for me. I had to concede that I was not making a very good start at a career, talent or no talent. Why not give it up?

Now I was so cast down by the words of one in whom I had been disappointed, whose very attitude I could not stomach, and it would take more than a little encouragement from another source before I should again feel that overwhelming urge to conquer the viola. I put the instrument in a closet the moment I reached Ohio and set out to find work, any kind of work, ready to heed my parents' advice. Did it have to be only music?

In my search for this "job," I went as far afield as I felt I could and still stay in Brilliant, the home of my parents at that time. So I found myself walking the streets of Pittsburgh one day, going to or from one more location that promised a job.

Suddenly, I heard myself hailed and, when I found the source of the call, recognized one of my Curtis friends, Bob Levine, whose home was in Dormont, a Pittsburgh suburb. We had played in one of Bailly's quartet classes during our time there. Upon hearing that I had given up the viola and was looking for any kind of work, Bob suggested that I reconsider my decision and get in touch with a Pittsburgh violinist who needed a violist for his quartet, the Yost Quartet.

Gaylord Yost was, like me, a product of the Midwest. His schooling as a musician had included a time spent in Europe, after which he returned to his own country for a career. At the moment, he was head of the Violin Department of the Pittsburgh Musical Institute, a position he had left Indianapolis to assume. Added to his laurels were his accomplishments as a composer, his works for the violin or string quartet being quite representative of the music of that era.

After considering my friend Bob's suggestion, I decided to at least investigate the possibility of Yost's quartet. I took my viola from the closet where it had lain for several months and tried my fingers and bow. I seemed to fall back into my old pre-Curtis groove and after several days of trial, I decided that just perhaps the idea had some merit. I could at least meet Yost and talk the matter over.

He was one to make a stranger feel at home, and as I played for him, I lost my nervousness and delivered some of my very best playing. He sketched the difficulties of the quartet's career in Pittsburgh and told me frankly that there was not a serious amount of money to be made with his group but asked if I would join with it in a cooperative endeavor. There was an amount of two thousand dollars pledged for the coming season for a series of five concerts, a final income of five hundred dollars per player when the pledges would have been collected. I really couldn't say no. Quartet playing was my real love, and I had really wanted, deep inside, a reason for returning to my viola.

With the quartet connection as a basis, I gave up thoughts of finding work outside the profession and looked within the musical activities of the Ohio Valley for engagements that might make it worthwhile to dedicate myself again to my instrument. They were available, though not remunerative in the true sense of the work. I was soon playing in the Wheeling Symphony, first viola, no less. Though I might be called the best violist in the ensemble, it was a relative rating, for all members were nonprofessionals who played for either their own pleasure or because they had been drafted to fill out the sections of the orchestra.

I found a place in a local string quartet and could count on a program about once a month with it. Since the conductor of the Wheeling Symphony was also the cellist of the quartet, there could be no conflict of dates, and the appearance of both orchestra and quartet were evenly spaced. For the quartet concert, I received $28; for the orchestra concert, $18, so my total income from these two sources was about $46 dollars per month, or a princely sum of about $11.50 per week.

Wheeling was about twenty-five miles from my parents' home, and Pittsburgh about sixty. The two weekly quartet rehearsals plus those of the orchestra kept me on the road a good part of my time.

In December of that year, the Boston Symphony was due to pay its annual visit to Pittsburgh. I was again in playing condition, and I resolved to ask for an audition with Serge Koussevitzky, its conductor. I remember arriving very early in the railroad station, seeking out the sleeping cars of the Symphony's train and awakening my old teacher as he slept in his berth. To my request that he ask Koussevitzky to let me play for him, he replied, "Humphrey, I would give my viola, even my wife, but do not ask me to do that for you!" He had his personal reasons that I did not insist on knowing. It was enough that he had refused me.

About midmorning, I asked the desk clerk at the Schenley Hotel if Koussevitzky was registered there. I was given his room number and found a house phone to make my call to him. As I gave the number, the telephone was taken from my hand—by Fourel who exclaimed, "If you are really so determined, I will do it for you!" And with that, it was done.

When I appeared before Koussevitzky, he was still in his bathrobe, his valet nearby unpacking his trunk. In such a relaxed atmosphere, there was considerable absence of the dignity for which he was noted. He sat and listened as I played my prepared work then questioned me as to my background. More than any other, the fact that I had studied at Curtis with the great Bailly impressed him. He was kindness itself as he explained that there was no vacancy at the moment, but he could promise that if I were to return to Boston, he would give me the first opportunity.

Now I really had something to work for!

The Yost Quartet gave its concerts, and the critics were kind to me and to the quartet. Yost and I had become warm friends, and I found the association an inspirational one. But with the final concert and counting of the monies collected from all sources, we could look at only $65! This was almost exactly the amount I had spent for gasoline to make my trips from Brilliant to Pittsburgh. My new colleagues could hardly do less than turn over the entire amount to me.

Of course, the Wheeling Symphony and quartet affiliations still gave me a slight income. But now I had the promised future with the Boston Symphony to hold me to the profession, and it seemed rather senseless to remain in the Valley when I might be back in Boston for the break of my opportunity.

As I revealed my plans to leave the Valley with the summer's end, my cellist-conductor colleague's attitude began to change. He saw the end of the quartet ahead, of course. My place in the symphony might be more easily filled than in the quartet, he knew, and there were just no capable violists about. I tried to disregard his mutterings as we rehearsed our quartet programs, but found it not so easy to turn my face during orchestra rehearsals when his dissatisfaction was more publicly displayed.

There came a moment, during a symphony rehearsal, when he shouted a foul name at me. I rose to answer him; he shoved me backward and reached for the nearest thing at hand. It was a trombone, and as he lifted it, the slide bent at an angle. He threw it down and took another, bending its slide also in his anger. We were both held by strong hands, and I was "assisted" to the outside hall from where I could look back and see him still fuming. So ended my career in Wheeling. I never saw my erstwhile colleague again.

Almost immediately, I set out again for Boston, but this time alone. I had written to the Conservatory and had been promised an amount of teaching that might assure me three meals daily and a place to stay. By now I had one son and another baby was soon expected, and it was best that I take my chances alone. My wife could best be cared for in my parents' home, I felt.

Even in 1932, the Depression had not relaxed its terrible hold on the city. Garbage pails were being ransacked for some little item that could be used in soup; desperate men were trying to sell apples on the city's street corners.

Enrollment at the Conservatory was small, and it was explained to me by the dean that the Jewish holidays were responsible. "Don't worry, George, in a few days things will loosen up, and you will see that I am keeping my word to you," said he. But things did not loosen up, and as the weeks crawled slowly by I knew that there was to be no class for me.

I used the last of the twenty-five dollars I had brought with me from Ohio and knew that I must now take any kind of work I could find. I answered a window ad and secured a position as dishwasher in the Arena Restaurant on the corner of St. Botolph Street and Massachusetts Avenue. At least I was sure of my meals, but there was no salary attached. My room rent, through the kindness of the landlady, was allowed to go on the cuff until I should see my way clear.

I had gained a bit of a reputation as a quartet player while at the Conservatory, and my mania for ensemble music was well known. I had hardly returned to Boston before I was invited to join with other players in chamber music sessions. They, like myself, had been forced into idleness and rather than put in boring hours practicing their instruments, gathered together to read the classics or familiarize themselves with the newer chamber music literature. For me, it was the perfect answer to my need for just that sort of activity.

I accepted the first invitation and soon found myself among players very well equipped for their tasks. There were several excellent violinists, two or three cellists, and an outstanding pianist who could not only read scores directly but transpose them at sight. The guiding spirit of these sessions was a clarinetist, Rosario Mazzeo, later of the Boston Symphony, in whose apartment they were held. There were flutists, bassoonists, oboists as well as horn players, and of course, contrabassists. I was one of two violists at first, but the other violist had a regular engagement in the local radio station and was more absent than not, so I took on the task of playing everything from duos to octets or even larger combinations when we had the players to handle such works.

Beginning at noon, players were free to drop in at Mazzeo's apart. and take part in whatever work could use their services. These chamber music marathons had to end about midnight, however, out of consideration for Mazzeo's neighbors.

From these sessions, I took much. I enlarged my own repertoire, evaluated myself as a player, and learned that there was seemingly no limit to my capacity or enthusiasm for such sessions. In time, certain players tended to group together with certain other players.

Eventually, a fairly constant string quartet evolved, and we found ourselves looking forward to our sessions as a unit. The cellist of the group, Josef Zimbler, very early showed strong business ability, so to him fell the chore of tracking down any possibility, however remote, that might give us an occasional fee. However, we continued the chamber music sessions with others, and I kept my job as a dishwasher, running from the sink to Mazzeo's apartment for even an hour or so of playing.

One session stands out in my memory. It began at seven o'clock one evening and went continuously until midnight when a break was called. Sandwiches were sent for, and we had a snack. At one o'clock, we began again and continued until 5 a.m. There were moments when we were playing Haydn quartets with flute, violin, viola, and horn!

Zimbler was successful. He sold the quartet idea to John Shepard of the Shepard Stores, who also owned radio station WNAC. Almost immediately, we were on the air as the Boston String Quartet and the Boston Chamber Music Ensemble. The quartet programs featured the four players; the ensemble programs used, in addition to the quartet, our score-reading pianist friend and a contrabassist. The quartet stayed within the classic literature as far as Beethoven, though we now and then played various fine transcriptions or arrangements as they were needed. The larger group assayed almost anything from Bach to Wagner, with occasional solo bits for each of us.

Our contract called for a one-half-hour program from each group six days a week. Obviously, much rehearsal time was necessary. I can recall, almost with disbelief, that we still continued to sit in on those ongoing chamber music marathons, and to this day I still believe that they, more than any other happenings, contributed to my skill as a chamber music violist.

No more dishwashing! I was once again on the true path, and I could congratulate myself that I had had the grit to overcome the obstacles I had found in my way. Now I could think of bringing my family to Boston; by this time there was another son to think of. I queried Zimbler, after we had been on the air several weeks, as to the length of time he thought we would be with the station. Together we went to see John Shepard and were told that he hoped we would go on and on, for judging by the letters received by the station, we were very popular.

So I sent for my family and waited out the days before they would arrive. Ten days elapsed before I found myself at the station watching their train pull in. I took my wife and our two sons to the apartment I had rented on a street off the Fenway, not too far from WNAC, and after seeing them settled, I continued on to rehearse and play our programs for the day. As we rehearsed, a letter was handed to Zimbler, and as he read it, his face became ashen. We were being given, for economic reasons, a two-week notice that we were through at the station, said he.

Now I was really in trouble. There was no longer a job, but there was a strong need to feed four mouths and provide a place for all of us to live. I had managed to put aside a few dollars from the work I had done with the quartet, and there was still a chance that a salary might allow me to put aside a bit more for the future. And we held on to a hope that we might be asked to continue, if only as a quartet.

I located a low-rent apartment in Medford, just outside Boston. The rent was $28 per month, and I thought that with luck I might be able to meet it. Of necessity, I joined the rolls of those who would do anything musical to make a dollar. Thus I was now not only a chamber music player, but one who was not too proud to engage in any legitimate musical endeavor.

Our broadcasts had attracted the attention of the conductor of the orchestra of the Metropolitan Theater. His name was Fabien Sevitzky, and he was a nephew of Serge Koussevitzky, the Boston Symphony's conductor, his name having been shortened for professional reasons. He was attempting to become a symphony conductor and, as a first step, had offered to revive the Peoples' Symphony, an organization made up of union musicians who wished to play music of a higher standard than they usually performed. A series of perhaps ten concerts brought in an amount that was shared cooperatively, at least in happy theory. Sevitzky sent for the quartet and asked us to join with him in reviving the almost dead Peoples'. He promised nothing but excellent "experience," but intimated that he could throw certain weeks of work our way in his Metropolitan Theater Orchestra.

Our second violinist had found a position at the Ritz Carlton Hotel, playing in the Tea Sessions; our first violinist had a heart condition that prohibited his taking on any more work than he could reasonably do. He had only stayed with the quartet because he enjoyed it and hadn't wished to jeopardize our chances by pulling out of the group. But Zimbler and I were free and willing to join Sevitzky. We told him that we would play in the Peoples' if he allowed us to be leaders of our respective sections. We felt that we wanted something from what we were about to do. Sevitzky agreed, and we joined forces.

He was as good as his word. He saw that each of us had an occasional week in the theatre, at a salary of $84. Even an infrequent amount of that size helped matters. But I couldn't feed my family on it.

Fortunately, there would be an occasional, very occasional, engagement at the opera house when a visiting company would attempt to foist its operatic wares on an unsuspecting public. And there was even a show now and then that could use my services in one theater or another. At one moment, I found myself playing violin for a debutante party with Ruby Newman's Orchestra—in New York. The engagement included nine hours of playing, with but a fifteen-minute rest period, plus the trip both ways in cars without heat, frozen up because of temperatures as low as sixteen degrees below zero. I remember that this engagement paid $46. It took me several days to recuperate from that ordeal!

Although the concerts of the Peoples' Symphony were well played, we were overshadowed by the concerts given at Symphony Hall, located almost across the street from our Jordan Hall, where the Boston Symphony answered the demands of Sevitzky's uncle, Serge. Our programs were spaced about three weeks apart, weeks necessary for rehearsing the works we would play. It seemed quite unfortunate that several times, only one week before our performances, the Symphony would play our to-be-featured work!

Near the end of the Peoples' season, I was pressed into service with the Metropolitan's orchestra for a week with Roxy, the impresario who had made such a reputation some years before in New York. He was going on the road with singers from his Roxy's Gang and would be making Boston his first stop. His troupe included not only Viola Philo and Robert Weede but a new singer named Jan Peerce. Peerce would be singing in public for the first time! Roxy would conduct.

At the end of the weeks' engagement with Roxy, he took me aside and asked me where I played. When he learned that I had no job, he suggested that I come to New York and accept a place in the orchestra he was forming for the reopening of the theatre that had seen him find fame. I couldn't refuse! He confided that he was just beginning his tour and would be gone six weeks: the next week in the Paramount Theatre in New York, then on to other cities. He asked me to see him during the coming week. I prepared to stay out the six weeks of his absence in New York while I got myself properly settled in with the union.

Those weeks in New York were to be some of the most miserable I have had to endure. On top of the troubles I encountered with union officials, I had my own economic problem to contend with. Half of the amount I had gotten together in Boston had to stay with my wife, and I had the other half with me—$25. I found an old friend who gave me sleeping space he shared with another if I came in after 11:00 p.m. and vacated before 7:00 a.m. to avoid a suspicious janitor. I could only drop in on him at certain times during the day when he was not at work and perhaps snatch time for a bit of scale playing! A Chinese restaurant just across the street from this attic apartment provided meals consisting mostly of rice. In an effort to conserve my dwindling resources, I sometimes spent but 50¢ per day, possible in those dark days of the Depression.

But I was making it through—until one day I saw a headline, "Roxy Drops Dead in Philadelphia!"

My wait was over. In my despair, I made up my mind to return to Boston, forsake music, and look again for a vocation that would at least provide some of the necessities, if not the luxuries, of life.

Though those were time-marking days for me, that spring in New York, elsewhere they were days of great activity. In Washington, Franklin D. Roosevelt's first administration was grasping at any straw that might point the way to a business recovery or to any means that might halt the descent of our peoples' morale. A dole under another name would be more palatable and preserve the dignity of the individual, of course, and so Roosevelt's New Deal conceived the National Relief Administration, the NRA; the Office of Price Administration, the OPA; the Emergency Relief Administration, the ERA, to name but a few of the host of bureaus created to allay our fears against fear itself. Each set of initials ended in the letter A, testifying to the fact that its bureau should be thought of as an administration. So common became our use of these sets of initials that the era has been called our alphabet days.

I arrived back in Boston to learn of the ERA, the Emergency Relief Administration, one of those set up to give immediate work and pay to the needy. Practically all professions or endeavors were eligible to share its benefits, and musicians descended on the offices that parceled out its employment benefits. Inquiry assured me that I was eligible for my share of its allotment, to the tune of $18 per week. My inherited trait of self-sufficiency had to take a back place in my thinking. The $18 per week was far more important. My dignity must suffer!

Only a few of Boston's musicians were able to stay clear of the ERA. As a consequence, the orchestras formed under the administration were made up of the city's best players, outside the Boston Symphony, of course, and the level of performance could be high. Soloists, chamber music players, orchestra players—all came within the scope of the ERA. I joined one of the large orchestras, to play first viola, and spent the next four months in that activity.

Though we performed primarily the literature of the symphony orchestra, there were other demands on us. We were expected to accompany any soloist thought good enough to perform his specialty in public. One name has stayed with me, that of a young lady of gorgeous appearance and voice, who seemingly had an unlimited capacity to learn and perform new vocal works or the standard arias of the operatic literature. Talented she was, and to prove it, Eleanor Steber was to go on to membership in the Metropolitan Opera.

The ERA was only a stopgap, I knew, and I knew that after its benefits had run out, the future still had to be faced. This temporary lifeline, however, served to keep me within the musical circle, and I had to practice daily to do the work it asked of me.

I returned to Boston from my six weeks in New York with the determination that I should make a last great effort to make my way as a musician, for otherwise I should be compelled to seek other means of livelihood to find a way to support my family, which included my wife and two young sons.

Toward that moment when the die should be finally cast, I began to prepare myself for a special audition with Serge Koussevitzky, the conductor of the world's greatest orchestra, the Boston Symphony. The vehicle I chose was one of the solo violin sonatas of J. S. Bach, which included one of his famous fugues for violin alone. Long and hard did I practice during the months of that summer.

I watched the newspapers that September and one day learned that Serge Koussevitzky had arrived in Boston after a summer in Europe. Feeling that he would shortly visit Symphony Hall, I waited one day and then approached Symphony Hall myself. I found my way to the orchestra library, then under the total supervision of one Leslie Rogers. According to all knowledge I had been able to glean, Rogers almost ran the orchestra, being at once librarian, personnel manager, program arranger, etc., etc.

I met Rogers for the very first time at that moment. To his question of what I wished, I answered, "I would like to play an audition for Koussevitzky." Learning that I had no appointment, he simply suggested that I get lost, especially since there was no vacancy in the viola section at that moment. I was expected to dismiss myself through the door he indicated. So through it I passed, into a corridor that I had learned led to Koussevitzky's private dressing room. Taking my courage in my hands, I simply walked to his door and knocked. As I knocked, I felt a hand on my shoulder and the voice of Rogers, "I thought I told you to get out." At that very moment, the door of the room opened, and there stood the man I wished to play for.

"Yes, vot is it?"

"I would like to play my viola for you."

"But my dear, ve haf no vacancy in the viola section."

"I know, but I wish you to remember me."

"Ah, yes. But ve haf met before . . . in Pittsburgh, and very good it vas. Please come in."

Leaving the befuddled Rogers, I entered and took the seat offered by Koussevitzky.

During our short conversation, I reminded him of his promise of several years before, and I told him I was keeping myself ready for such a vacancy when and if it might exist. There had been no vacancy since I had last played for him, Koussevitzky told me, "But you are here. Vy you don't blay?"

Then he said, "Vot you vish to blay?"

"A Bach sonata I have prepared for you."

"Please, no Bach. Vot else do you haf?"

"I have brought nothing else."

With that, Koussevitzky summoned Rogers and asked him what cello sonatas might be in the library. Rogers answered that there was a sonata by Sammartini. I breathed a sigh of relief for this sonata was known to me, one of those works that is always remembered if one has ever studied it.

"But ve must haf it a pianist. Is Fiedler here?" Rogers said that Fiedler was in the library. Koussevitzky suggested that I go and get him.

Thus I met Arthur Fiedler for the first time. When I approached him with a request that he accompany my audition, he simply asked, "What are you playing? How fast does it go?" He then joined me as I returned to Koussevitzky's room.

The first movement went without incident. My memory played me no tricks. We went on to the second movement, a lovely singing lento, as I recall. When we had finished, Koussevitzky said, "Now I vill conduct." And conduct he did. We returned to the slow movement, and he led me through it, bending every phrase, indicating rubato I had not used before. Certain notes were elongated, while others were shortened. He smiled as we found our way to the end, realizing that I knew what he was doing, deliberately distorting the music to test my ability to follow him.

When we had finished, Koussevitzky smiled and said, "You see, many things can be done with the music. Very good!" Then he asked me if I wondered why he knew this sonata so well. I had no idea, and he revealed to me that it was one of those he had used so successfully during his recitals as a bass soloist in the years when he had amassed a huge reputation as the foremost exponent of that so cumbersome instrument.

While I had been playing, Koussevitzky had sent for George E. Judd, then manager of the orchestra. Mr. Judd stood listening, a look of surprise on his face. What in the world was Koussevitzky up to? He was soon to learn.

"I vant this man in my orchestra. Please give him contract!"

"This is impossible. The orchestra has just accepted cuts in salaries. Our budget will not permit it."

"I vill go to the trustees. Please."

"I will have to look over the situation. I will see."

The audition took place on a Tuesday morning. First rehearsals of the orchestra would start the following Monday. I left the audition with great hopes in my heart. Days passed, and I heard nothing. I was afraid to forsake our apartment for fear that the telephone might summon me, and I would not be there to answer my call to duty in the Symphony. Four days went by and my inner tension mounted.

Finally, on the following Sunday evening, I summoned up my courage and reached Mr. Judd at his home in Norwell. All I got from him was an invitation to have a chat with him at 9:30 the next morning in Symphony Hall. I went prepared, my viola resting beside me as we sat talking together. He extolled the beauties of his Norwell flower garden. He asked if I had visited the exhibits then in view at Horticultural Hall, just across the street. Finally, with nothing more of small talk to explain our meeting, Mr. Judd suggested that since Mr. Koussevitzky seemed determined to have me in the orchestra there was nothing to do but give me a chance.

He offered me the thirty-week season of employment with the Symphony, but would have to withhold the Pops season for the first year. If I pleased Koussevitzky in that first season, I could expect my second to include Pops also. I literally had no choice, for it was again dinned into me that there was no vacancy, and that I should be the thirteenth violist, a position never before existing in the orchestra. I signed my name to a contract. And so it began.

By this time, it was only ten minutes until the beginning of the first rehearsal. No time to spare! In that last hurried moment, a place on the stage had to be found for me. Where normally twelve players sat, thirteen had to be placed. I was directed to sit between my teacher, Georges Fourel, a Frenchman, and Carl Barth, a very typical German of an older school, between the viola and cello sections, with no time to wonder about anything but my own necessity to produce the results expected of me by Koussevitzky.

Amid a sudden hush, Koussevitzky strode to the podium, bowed to the applause that greeted him, and then stepped up on the podium. Excitedly, I waited for the words that would come from the man who had so suddenly assumed so large a place in my personal and professional life.

After introducing the several new players, of which I was one, he launched into a speech of greeting. "So ve haf accomplished this great vork in the ten years I haf been here . . . and I hopes to remain another ten years to go on with the great vork ve haf begun . . ."

There was an uncomfortable pause while he took time to fix with his eye every member of the orchestra, beginning with the concertmaster, Richard Burgin, and progressing through every section. There was no hurry evident, and he would pause until each player looked at him. "But some of you vill not!"

I was not neglected in this wholesale scrutiny, and I felt anything but comfortable. But there was no time to dwell on my own discomfort, and I could take refuge in the knowledge that I was only there at all because *he* wanted me in his orchestra.

I could never forget that first rehearsal with the Boston Symphony if I were to live a thousand years! The manner of my arrival there, the moment itself, and the later conflicts within me that were to result are reason enough for it to be an unforgettable moment. The immediate emotion I felt was that of relief and thankfulness to be suddenly freed of the Depression, so to speak, freed of the darkness of mood that accompanied those days of wandering streets, here and elsewhere, seeking always the place I hoped might be waiting for me in my chosen profession, and to be at last on the path of my life's work. Close on the heels of that first emotion was the elation that came from knowing I was actually a member of the orchestra the world regarded as the foremost ensemble of the day.

It was one thing to be a member of one of our better-known Midwestern orchestras as a member of the viola section. It was another to be a member of an ERA group in which I played solo viola. Even a higher level of accomplishment, at least musically, was my involvement with the Peoples' Symphony, where I also led the viola section. It might be inferred that my musical pleasure was gauged by my personal responsibilities in a group. Perhaps so, yet I was soon to recognize this moment to be the highest point in my musical career to date, though I was not playing first viola but was merely the unnecessary thirteenth violist of the section.

I was unprepared for the sweep of sound from this body of virtuoso performers, any of whom, I already felt, could show me cards and spades. I was carried along in this stream of golden sound. These men were playing the notes before them as though they had lived with them for years of their lives, as indeed some of them had. Over this fine body of players, one spirit was presiding, and I was now experiencing that peculiar hypnotism exerted by this man from whom it emanated. In the years I was to spend under his baton, I was to see no lessening of his power to sway his players. Much too soon came the end of this, my first rehearsal with the Boston Symphony.

Koussevitzky was the conductor in every sense the word implies. There could be no room for more than one controlling hand, and it had to be his. He had come to Boston with the determination to build its orchestra into the finest the world had ever seen, and to this task he had dedicated his knowledge, strength, and energy, brooking no interference from any direction. These considerations had been in his mind when he made his opening speech at my first rehearsal. I was never to see one moment when a wavering from this pledge to himself might be indicated.

In Boston, he had found an orchestra made up of players generally of Germanic background, steeped in the tradition of that country's music and its manner of performance. Dr. Karl Muck, admittedly one of the world's finest conductors, had built from these players an orchestra tremendous in their ensemble. Muck had been forced to vacate his position in 1918 and return to his native Germany. His immediate successor, Henri Rabaud of France, stayed but one season to be succeeded by Pierre Monteux, also a Frenchman. Monteux mounted the podium in 1919. He had not yet attained his full stature as a conductor and lacked the ability to be a disciplinarian.

In the five years of his conductorship, he had been unable to stem the antagonistic feeling and could do little more than hold the status quo of a lower level of performance. When Koussevitzky arrived in Boston in 1924, discipline was at a low ebb, and the average age of the players had advanced with a consequent deterioration of their abilities to perform. Still there was the feeling of resentment against anyone who might attempt to turn the orchestra from its Muckian ways.

It took Koussevitzky only part of a season to make his feelings felt. Some players were asked to resign, some dismissed, and still others, feeling the future upon them, simply left the orchestra to avoid the stigma of being requested to terminate their memberships.

In his second season, Koussevitzky had filled vacated positions with several players from the Paris Conservatoire. He was to continue the practice through those first half-score years, until at the moment of my arrival the orchestra was about evenly divided between German and French players. Such a situation could not be expected to be a harmonious one, save in the purely musical sense. Traditionally, these two countries have shown themselves to be at odds. It was not uncommon when a French classic was being rehearsed for mutterings to be heard from the German players who would not admit the existence or ability of Ravel, Debussy, or even Berlioz. These mutterings were duplicated by those Frenchmen who detested the sight of Brahms's name or the sound of his music. At times, even Beethoven had difficulty finding his way into their hearts.

In between these factions now stood a conductor of still another nationality. That he was Russian set him apart from either side of this age-old controversy, yet it made him vulnerable from both sides. It took only a slight difference in the interpretation of a French masterpiece to ruffle the Frenchmen; similarly the Germans could point to a host of misinterpretations of a famous German classic.

His position could not help being difficult! A conductor who faces an orchestra made up of members of the same national persuasion has a formidable task when he attempts to have them play together. Place him before a body of men who have been long-standing members of one of the world's best orchestras and who have played many of those years under one of the world's best conductors. Let him replace their fallen comrades with players of a traditionally different ideology. Then let him expose the ensemble to a repertoire largely new to most of them, with more than a small number of compositions being given their first performances, with consistent tedious rehearsals demanded of each player, new or old, that he find new ways to overcome the difficulties propounded by a new school of composers.

No one will deny that the conductor facing such conditions must have a hand of strength. Koussevitzky had this strong hand, and in addition a taste in music so catholic that he overrode all nationalistic boundaries and performed the music that he thought best represented the art to which he had given his life. It mattered not to him that another noted conductor or a famous composer had been willing to accept the sort of performance that was "good enough" for the work being performed. To him had been given the opportunity—heaven sent—to create something better than had ever been before, and he accepted the responsibility of the task with no reluctance.

He had risen from the ranks of his Russian ancestry through his own musical genius and had, before he found his place as a conductor, firmly established himself as perhaps the leading contrabass virtuoso of the world of the early twentieth century. From a beginning as conductor of an orchestra that toured up and down the Volga River about 1912, he had risen to European fame through his Concerts Koussevitzky in Paris before accepting the post in Boston.

Undoubtedly, his earlier choice of the contrabass as his instrument influenced him in his fight for an orchestral tone unlike any other in the world. The bottom of his orchestral sounds was that of the contrabasses, and they had to be grand indeed, else there would be an examination of his bass section, even its individual players until he would ferret out the culprit or the circumstances that interfered with the beauty of the sound as he conceived it.

This examination of the sections and its individuals was not confined to the bass section alone, but included all the sections of the orchestra. He believed the strings of the orchestra to be the foundation of all sounds produced by it and seemed never to be completely satisfied with their efforts, except perhaps on very special occasions. Small wonder that no string player was ever tempted to ride along without daily practice on his instrument.

It would be rather difficult to explain completely Koussevitzky's conductorial technique. It was almost entirely a personal thing and was not necessarily patterned after any other conductor's. I was to hear him say, at a later date, that his idol had been Arthur Nikisch, a former conductor of the Boston Symphony, who had been known as the Poet of the Baton. Nikisch had gone on to a greater European fame, and it was during that time in his career that Koussevitzky had taken notice of him.

Koussevitzky's baton was a very short delicate stick, almost merely an extension of his index finger. He wielded it with great finesse and exquisite delicacy, yet still it was not sufficient to impart his ideas, so he demanded and got rehearsals that would give him sufficient time to explain what it was he wanted. During those many rehearsal hours, he tried one way or another to reach that pinnacle of interpretation he conceived in his mind. Above all, he insisted on orchestral "color" at all times and could not accept any playing that did not give those vivid hues of tone he heard in his head.

The orchestra had difficulty in following his baton at times. He was very vague, at times, in giving a clear indication of just when to begin sound. "Personne must know vere it begin," he would say. He had a habit of lifting the baton to its proper height for a beginning, then bringing it down ever so slowly without a perceptible bottom to its movement. A player cannot begin to play unless he knows just when the bottom of the beat has been reached. I can recall a moment when he was asked to explain where the bottom of his beat was, the wind players having difficulty with a piano attack. "Ven I strike the air, dot is my beat," was his reply.

Yet this vagueness had caused the orchestra to gain the virtuosity of a huge ensemble, a quality missing in any orchestra of the time, at least in America. Listeners were often to ask us how, in heaven's name, we ever followed the stick, and it was very hard to explain that in the moment of first attack, each player was cautious not to be the first to play. The split second that elapsed after a player heard another play and then played himself was not discernible to the average listener. This was occasionally carried to almost ludicrous extremes when Koussevitzky had advanced into the second beat of his music before anyone had gained enough nerve to make the first sound.

At certain very, very critical moments, the orchestra would look to Richard Burgin, the concertmaster, and watch for his bow to begin its stroke. If the wind sections were to begin alone, the key figure was Georges Laurent, first flutist. A certain muscular action in the back of his neck gave the signal of when he was about to begin. It was possible, then, for the orchestra to play without that stiffness of beat many conductors employ, thus allowing Koussevitzky to indulge his poetic pleasure in molding the music to his desires.

A player new to the ensemble, as I was, could not know immediately the differences between Koussevitzky's conducting and that of the conductors he may have played with. It had to grow on you. My first season was also the first for the new bass trombone player. For weeks, he was completely ahead of the orchestra and was completely right; the rest of us were wrong, but wrong together, which made his rightness wrong.

As the thirteenth violist, I was considered a problem, if not musically, at least physically, for the section had its accustomed place on the stage, and I was a new element hard to absorb. During the coming weeks, I would be, in one work, comfortably seated between the second stands of the viola and cello sections, the position in which I had first been placed. In another I would be squeezed in, far back beside the harps, almost out of communication with my section. I shuttled back and forth, my placement being determined by the size of the stage, the instruments used in a work, or even the absence of another violist, whose place I was expected to take. I was the "floater" of the section, expected to play any divisi part on any stand should occasion require.

Of course, this indeterminate status was to contribute vastly to my orchestral experience, for the necessity of always being prepared gave me no time to rest on past accomplishments, but forced me to make myself familiar with any or all parts that might be put before me. There were to be many instances when I would be called to perform in a work I had not even rehearsed due to Koussevitzky's habit of cutting the orchestra down in works of Bach, Haydn, or Mozart. Those were tense moments for me, and I quickly discovered that this man who had been so kind to me offstage seemingly had no friends when he was in performance. And I could not expect to be immune from the glance of displeasure he gave the orchestra when things had not gone exactly to his liking.

Koussevitzky appeared large when he stood in his place on the podium. Actually, he was perhaps five feet seven inches tall, but he carried himself very straight and had kept his youthful slimness of figure. He had a quiet dignity about him, and his figure was clothed in what was often called sartorial elegance, a fortunate choice of tailor having more than a little to do with it, no doubt.

There was an electric quality about him that was evident when he made his first step through the door to the stage. When that door opened, an entire audience came erect, total quiet immediately fell, and his appearance was awaited with excitement. His path led behind the viola and harp sections, five steps to the corner of the risers, where he turned right and took eight more steps, these bringing him to the center of the stage. Every one of those thirteen steps was taken with unhurried dignity, and when he reached his central position, he made a very courtly bow before mounting the podium. There was not a doubt that here was the king about to hold court, his speeches to be made in the medium closest to his heart.

CHAPTER 2

The Koussevitzky Years

At the time I began my tenure with the Boston Symphony, the personnel was about evenly divided between French and German players, some others of European extraction, and about six who might be called real Americans, having been born and reared here. That would now include myself, and so I joined that small group that had earned the title of Yankees.

But regardless of where they had originated, the spirits of the players were extremely high, as was their ability to accomplish what was asked of them. It cannot be denied that there was a large element of fear involved, for Koussevitzky was the complete autocrat, a dictator of a kind, who insisted on nothing but the best of what each player could bring to his task. He had been determined to make of the Boston Symphony the greatest group the world had ever known, and he had succeeded to the point where the reputation of the orchestra was worldwide and admitted to be exactly what he had hoped. All knew that his words during his speech were not of an idle nature, and none wished to be the recipient of his wrath.

Almost at once, as we rehearsed Richard Strauss's *Also sprach Zarathustra*, Koussevitzky spoke to that excellent timpanist, A. Ritter, who had joined the orchestra in 1922. Koussevitzky had become its leader in 1924.

"Ritter, ve haf been togedder now ten years, and in all that time, you haf made only three mistakes—but two of them last year." Ritter took the hint and resigned at the end of that 1934-1935 season. His resignation caused a vacancy in the percussion section. Knowing that Richard Burgin, our concertmaster, was to make a visit to Poland during the coming summer, Koussevitzky spoke to him in this wise, "Richard, I remember a fine timpanist from Warsaw who played

---

35

with me several years ago. I cannot remember his name. See if you can find this man and ask him to join our orchestra." Burgin was able to learn the name of this timpanist, asked him how his muscles were holding up, and being assured that he felt very well, asked this fine player if he would care to come to Boston. Thus we procured Roman Szulc without formal audition!

Since its inception, the orchestra had been completely nonunion. From a splendid board of trustees had come gentlemen's agreements that had made the playing and living conditions of the orchestra members superior to those of any like organization in this and probably other countries as well. The players enjoyed the prestige of membership and were thus welcomed into many organizations in Boston as well as into many homes they might otherwise never have seen. They lived a life apart, except for their common interest in what they had to do while on the stage of Symphony Hall. There Koussevitzky reigned supreme, almost dictating their very lives, for to him they owed complete subjugation. What he said was final, not always completely fair and just, many thought, but necessarily regarded as the last word from him who controlled their very lives.

Though Koussevitzky had a compelling way with much of the world's musical masterpieces, his particular forte was said to be the music of Russia, the country of his birth and childhood. More particularly, the music of Tchaikovsky had come to be considered his specialty, though works of Rimsky-Korsakoff, Rachmaninoff, and later, Shostakovich were all given their due. He seemed most fond of the Sixth Symphony of Tchaikovsky, the *Pathétique*, and his frequent use of it and his very personal handling of it had caused him to be considered its most loving interpreter. In the ten years already gone, the *Pathétique* had probably had more individual performances than any other single work. It could be that this total familiarity of conductor and orchestra with the *Pathétique* was to blame for an incident that took place several weeks after I had joined the viola section.

Announced for the coming weekend's program was one work that the orchestra had played before—in a different version—some years previously. Aaron Copland had written a symphony for organ and orchestra that had been performed with Nadia Boulanger, Copland's famous Parisian composition master, during one of her early visits to Boston. Now Copland had rescored the work for orchestra alone and was calling it his Symphony no. 1 (revised). In my normal habit of looking all parts over in advance, I had taken the part home.

In my attempts to fathom its difficulties, I had discovered what I thought to be an error of notation in the viola part. As I came to the hall for the Monday night concert, I brought the offending part to the library and queried the orchestra's librarian, Mr. Rogers, as to its correctness. We consulted the score and determined that there was indeed an error that should be immediately corrected. The orchestra's librarian, now much friendlier to me, wrote a note and placed it in Koussevitzky's score so that he might inform the violists at the next morning's rehearsal before they had a chance to waste time in finding the error. My part was corrected on the spot.

That Monday night concert began with the Prelude to Moussorgsky's *Khovanshchina*, a short work always included in a program that featured the *Pathétique*. Debussy's *La mer* would take us up to intermission. The *Pathétique* would conclude the program.

The viola section was always in a nervous state when the Prelude was to be played, for the violas had to begin it on a third beat that was often more poetic than clear due to Koussevitzky's preoccupation with the beauty of the work itself. Also, worse to come, were those soloist passages for the violas in the Tchaikovsky work, during which the conductor seemed to fix each player with his eye and demand from him the greatest beauty of sound "die the vorld has heard" in every note of the phrase.

Fortunately, the *Khovanschina* got off to good start, and the viola section breathed again, disaster having been avoided at least temporarily. I have no memory of the performance of *La mer* being below the orchestra's high standard of excellence.

After intermission, the *Pathétique* began with its pianissimo double bass and bassoon utterances of coming themes. This particular symphony, after the first few measures of introduction, then actually begins with a theme that is given out by a divided viola section, half playing a solo and the other half assisting them when necessary. But where we had expected a strong baton beat, necessary to hold us together in our divided melodies, we got only a rather nebulous gesture, almost circular in shape with no point or rhythmic pulse.

Thirteen men had thirteen different ideas of what was meant to be played, and the result was total disorder. I could not fasten my playing to anything I was hearing around me, and I could not find any firmness of beat from the conductor, at that moment livid with rage at what was happening. By the end of perhaps three measures, he had begun to beat savagely the strokes that would pull us together, and by the time the passage had come to its end, we were once again a section united.

During the rest of that long movement, Koussevitzky conducted, almost entirely, the viola section. We felt his eyes boring in on us, the anger prominently displayed on his face. For the rest of the symphony, even when we had nothing of importance, he conducted only us. As the concert ended, we were thirteen beaten men ready to slink from the stage and vanish forever into the night. As I accompanied my fellow violists from the stage, each one was explaining that Koussy was looking only at him. I knew better, for hadn't he looked *only at me*? And I had the terrible knowledge that this was the orchestra's first performance of the *Pathétique* with me, they having done it many times beautifully, long before I had appeared on the scene. I slept not a wink that night waiting for the next morning's denouement. I was sure to be once again at liberty to find my musical way.

The next morning, we all waited for the storm to break, but to our very great surprise, not a word was said, and rehearsal started as usual. We began with the Copland Symphony and made our way toward no. 37 with its incorrect measure (I can never forget its location). Of course, I expected the librarian's note to be read and the correction to be made when we had reached the spot. Instead, we were stopped and we heard, "You, you ruined my symphony last night!" One of the violists found the accusing finger pointing at him. "You rosh (rush)!" If there was anything to be said of this particular player, it was that he never rushed. He might occasionally lag, but he never rushed. His basal metabolism wouldn't have allowed it. Then, "Play at no. 37!" This poor chap with his years of experience and very good sight-reading ability had not taken the Copland part home and was seeing it for the first time. He played what he saw, and it was not correct, of course. Then Koussevitzky invited this player's desk mate to join with his colleague. As they muddled through the measure, not at all in agreement, Koussevitzky turned to the first stand and instructed them to play the measure. While they were coming to disaster, the rest of the section tensed toward the moment when we should be asked to play by stand or player alone.

I was sitting at that moment at the end of the section beside the sixth stand. I decided that when their turn should come, I would join them rather than be singled out for a solo. The moment came, and the three of us raised our violas. Suddenly, Koussevitzky changed his mind and said, "Alone, you play alone," and he pointed at me. I could not avoid the order and played what I had in my music, the corrected measure at no. 37.

In the meantime, Jean Le Franc, the first violist, had been looking at that measure and hearing what I did with it. He showed his part to Koussevitzky with, "But the measure is wrong in the music." He got the reply, "Ah, yes, but a fine player see at sight it is wrong, and he correct it!" This was not the kind of notice I had been seeking, and I had no intention of trying to show any player up. I had simply done the only thing left for me to do. Of course, I had done myself no harm.

It was a good week later, the performance of the Copland behind us, when suddenly, in the middle of rehearsal, Koussevitzky stopped, looked at us with a sly smile, and said, "You remember our fiasco of last veek?" (How could we ever forget it?) "I must tell you vot happen. After *La mer* come this young conductor to my room. He say, 'Your orchestra is magnificent, particularly the string sections. Tell me, Maestro, vot do you think is your best section?' And I say, 'My violas; listen and you vill hear!' And he listen, and you know vot he hear!" The young conductor was Artur Rodziński. There was a suspicion that in an attempt to astound this young man, our conductor had indulged his fancies beyond our understanding.

Thirteen good men breathed sighs of relief to know that the fiasco was not being put to their personal discredit.

Koussevitzky's treatment of the *Pathétique* had made it a work associated with his name beyond that of all others. He injected into its performance all the ardor and the love of its Russian meanings (to him) of which he was capable. But of all the small changes he had managed to include, there is one that stands out above all others. Very close to the end of the work, there is a stroke of the tam-tam that can be viewed as a climax of a kind or just a passing moment. Koussevitzky preferred to consider this tam-tam stroke as the real climax (the culmination of the "contrapuntical themes," as he put it) of the piece. Never a rehearsal, but he used a few moments to inspect the manner in which the tam-tam was to be struck. In very frequent instances, he would walk through the orchestra, take the stick in his hand, and play the tam-tam in the way he wished it to be played. Never did it occur to him, I am sure, that he was not following his own beat and so could be at ease when he struck the gong.

Immediately following the tam-tam stroke, a small pause was always made to allow the tam-tam to ring in its full majesty. Then the trombones were to intone beautiful chords. Almost without variation, so much was made of the tam-tam stroke that the players in the trombone section were frightened beyond proportion by the difficulty of their task. Their entrance would be ragged, their rhythm faulty and insecure, to the point of drawing scowls from the conductor.

We were giving a concert in Baltimore. The stage of the Lyric Theatre was so shallow that very high risers had been used, risers that placed the percussion section very much higher than was customary. The percussionists were in the back of the stage and seemingly far above us. The tam-tam hung in its accustomed place.

The grand moment came. In accordance with Koussevitzky's wish, it was struck by Max Polster, and the resultant sound was not less beautiful than desired. But the rawhide thong holding the gong in its position within the steel framework in which it usually hung, broke, and it dropped to the floor with another boom not in the score. Pausing upright for an instant, it then rolled and dropped to the next riser, another boom coming from it. The forward motion continued and with each drop to the next riser, it continued its solo. Its path was through the second violin section, and as it reached Ralph Del Sordo, he yelled, "Jesus Christ!" and swung out of its way. Straight ahead it continued, booming as it went, until it had reached the floor, somewhat more level than had been the risers. There, its motion almost at a standstill, it rolled slowly until it had hit the small riser on which Koussevitzky stood. It settled to the stage with an infernal clatter directly in front of Koussevitzky.

In the meantime, the audience had become hysterical, the orchestra likewise, to the point where anything resembling the sublime moments with which the

Pathétique ends had ceased to exist. Koussevitzky was beside himself with rage, and the end of the symphony was nothing like it had usually been. When he left the stage, he failed to return.

But there were other conclusions to this symphony that would be much harder to explain. At its end, in Carnegie Hall ("Personne must know ven it ends"), there stood Koussevitzky bent over the score. No applause! No one dared to move. The orchestra sat in deep silence. Finally, Koussevitzky opened the fingers of his right hand, the baton fell onto the score, and he turned, stepped to the floor, and made four steps toward the wings before any one had the audacity to clap a hand. Mass hypnotism, without doubt!

Koussevitzky's manner of rehearsal was this: he entered the stage from the right side, dropping his Russian cloak into the hands of his valet, Victor. This black cloak, usually worn around his shoulders, was lined with the fur of some small animals. One of our cellists made bold to insinuate that these skins came from the rats he commonly ate for breakfast. Once through the door, he strode to his position in the center of the stage, gave a good morning, and proceeded to the task at hand. His concentration was complete, and nothing was allowed to disturb it. Only his voice was heard at any time. A question asked by him was not supposed to be answered unless asked twice. Such rhetorical questions were always to the point and left no one in doubt as to his meaning. Using the four languages with which he was somewhat conversant, he would concoct sentences to explain his meanings or to incite the orchestra to play the way he wished. His baton technique was such that it was necessary for him to attempt vocal instruction to explain his meaning. Rehearsals began at 10:00 a.m. and ended at 1:00 p.m. if all seemed well to him, but on occasion we might go much further. There were no rules except those laid down by Koussevitzky himself.

It could not happen again. In a day when the players of an orchestra are undoubtedly better equipped technically than they were at that time, the spirit of the players would rebel against any such "tyranny." Their unionization would allow them to prefer charges against anyone who was thought to be tyrannical, derogatory in his remarks, or who might very occasionally violate to a fraction some rule set up for a rehearsal's time limit.

Koussevitzky's rehearsals were supposed to last three hours, but it was not uncommon for Koussevitzky to continue with his rehearsal until well after the usual finishing time, even on some occasions until nearly two o'clock. Today, the overtime fees to be paid would seem exorbitant in the management's eyes, and they would no doubt frown on the practice.

His language was indeed descriptive. He might tell us: "You know vot to do."

"I see your bows move, but I don't haf nothing."

"Please, no died fingers!"

"Find the tempo and keep it."

"Mezzo forte is the most baddest nuance qui existe."

"Tradition! I hate it. Ve vill make our own tradition."

A moment later . . .

"But dot is the tradition of this music."

"Made of yourself a little machine. Like a votch."

"You must haf a bow one thousand kilo."

"I vill rehearse a thousand times until I vill not haf every note." (A confusion between the meaning of "until" and "while.")

"I rehearse for bedder, not badder."

"Ee don't go."

"To the last atom."

One never smiled at his remarks. It would have been fatal.

Shortly after my arrival, we had stayed on the stage in rehearsal until long after our usual time. It was about one forty or so, when suddenly pointing to a location in the back stands of the second violins, Koussevitzky ordered, "Take your violin and go." Several of the players in that area, unable to decide just who the offending player might be, whispered to each other, "Does he mean me?" Again came the order, and the players were able to pinpoint the man he meant. They whispered, "I think he means you, Sam!"

Sam rose from his chair and quietly removed himself. As he did so, Koussevitzky turned to Richard Burgin, our concertmaster, and asked, "Who is he? I cannot haf strangers in my orchestra." Sam had been caught by Koussevitzky's eye as he unconsciously let his violin slip from its usual high position. The length of rehearsal had brought on fatigue, causing the temporary lapse. Sam had only been in the orchestra for fourteen years! Of course he was allowed to return to his accustomed seat the next day, and he was to far outlast Koussevitzky in his tenure in the orchestra.

Koussevitzky's baton technique was anything but perfect. He was completely capable of beating the commonly used rhythms, but he had great difficulty in departing from them. Often a measure of five beats would be elongated to six, one of seven beats used up the time usually given to eight beats. Thus it was a task for the players to decide what to do with the passagework they were expected to play, and yet make their played notes fit the time the score allowed or the conductor asked for, often two different things.

His batons were very small, almost an elongation of his index finger. They were manufactured right there in the hall by one stage-manager or another in off moments. Never did Koussevitzky allow himself to be without his baton, for his very technique was founded on its use, and in that use he was elegant indeed.

I had been in the orchestra a few weeks when I became conscious of an expression frequently used by the players when speaking of another's accomplishments. "My boy, I have heard them all," was said often enough that even the words, "My boy," implied the rest of the sentence. Eventually, I learned its origin, and it seems to have sprung from the following incident.

One of our flutists, in his younger days as freelancer in Boston, had found it difficult to secure work, although he investigated every possibility of which he had news. Suddenly, he heard that a position for the summer was available in Newport, Rhode Island, a position ensuring ten full weeks of work. At that time, many of these summer engagements were under the control of John Mulally, a violist in the Symphony. At the same moment, Mulally had discovered that he himself was having a hard time finding a flutist for this engagement. Mulally was also the violist on the job, it being perhaps the most prestigious of those that he controlled. It seemed fortuitous to both parties that their problem could be solved by letting the young flutist have the position.

The weeks passed until at the end of the sixth, our young flutist could withhold his curiosity no longer. He went to see Mulally and nervously asked, "Mr. Mulally, I have been playing with you for six weeks, and in that time you have said nothing to me about my playing. What do you think of me?"

Mulally placed a hand on our young man's shoulder, and with the most benevolent expression, answered, "My boy, I have heard them all, and you are the worst. You do things even a child wouldn't do."

Still, our young flutist had persisted, practiced hard and eventually became the third flutist of the Boston Symphony. His duty was to assist in the tuttis and be ready to step in should sickness cause disruption in the section. We were beginning one of our Carnegie Hall concerts in New York when Georges Laurent, our first flutist, became ill and was unable to continue the program already in progress. The next work at hand was Debussy's, *Afternoon of a Faun*, a work featuring the flute with all of its difficulties musically and technically. Nothing was left but that our third flutist must take the position of Laurent and perform the work. Although our third flutist was not of the stature of Laurent, the playing was of good quality and the performance was a good one.

Back in Boston, Koussevitzky took a moment to speak of it, "A . . . I congrotulate you upon your playing of *de faun* in New York, but please, ven you make triller, do not toodle-oodle!" With that, the third flutist jumped to his feet and replied, with some heat, "I don't toodle-oodle." So fearsome did he appear in that moment that Koussevitzky turned and said to Burgin, "Gahngster!"

There was nothing erratic about Koussevitzky's beat. His rhythm was excellent, but his technique of beating ahead of the orchestral response to his commands caused a discrepancy between what the audience saw and what they heard. He was questioned by one of the more daring players as to just where the beat was. He replied, "Ven I strike de air, that is the beat." One of the prominent solo players had determined that Koussevitzky's baton descended to the bottom limit of his beat; then upon its rise, the beat coincided with the moment when it reached the fourth button on his vest. Anyone's guess was as good as another's.

In actual fact, the players seemed to operate thusly: wind players seated behind Georges Laurent, first flute, could tell when he was to play by watching the muscles of his neck. They learned to follow him in their attacks. String players could see when Richard Burgin, our concertmaster, was to stroke his strings and acted accordingly. Close collaboration between Burgin and Laurent created an ensemble sufficient for our needs. Added to that was the knowledge each player had of the score, gained from much rehearsal and many instructive words from the conductor. The orchestra had thus become a huge ensemble.

I recall that very early in my membership, an attempt was made to correct this visual and aural discrepancy. The work at hand was Richard Strauss's *Also sprach Zarathustra*. Normally, this work gives no difficulty, but Koussevitzky had a habit of winding himself up to deliver the beat of the large chords of this introduction. We were cautioned to "made of yourselves a little machine," so that we would be playing our chords in exact rhythm. There was an attempt to do exactly what Koussevitzky had asked, but only a brave soul would insist on following the instructions delivered by the conductor. Such a brave soul was Yves Chardon, second stand cellist. He did as requested and so played entirely alone to the consternation of all, especially Koussevitzky. But he was absolutely correct!

After one or two more of such trials on Koussevitzky's part and also on Chardon's, it was seen that wished-for and accomplished results were two different things. The subject never came up again. We played as before for a result not necessarily rhythmically correct, but nevertheless hair-raising. But Koussevitzky's baton technique was eloquent indeed. At some time earlier, he had taken as his model Artur Nikisch, a true poet of the baton, and had tried to pattern himself on this former conductor of the Boston Symphony. Nikisch had passed on to European triumphs.

Koussevitzky felt that he knew the Beethoven symphonies, but his players did not always feel that this was so. There is a moment in the Fifth when the oboe is asked to play a small cadenza. Jean Gillet's reading of these few notes was not to Koussevitzky's liking. Neither did Gillet agree with Koussevitzky's concept of the same passage. After a good deal of disagreement, almost acrimonious, Gillet, realizing that Koussevitzky must have his way in the end, suggested that, "Will you please conduct so that no one will blame me for what I do." So it was done.

In 1938, we learned about the possibility of the orchestra's making a tour of Russia and certain European centers. Koussevitzky was delighted at this chance to return with what he considered the greatest orchestra in the world to the land of his youth, a chance to show what he had accomplished since his departure. The matter was discussed quite amicably until it was revealed that we would be expected to fly across the ocean. That spelled defeat for the idea. The members voted not to undertake the dangerous gamble, much to the conductor's chagrin. Still, he made little of it. No doubt he had other things on his mind: Tanglewood, for instance.

In 1936, the orchestra gave concerts in Holmwood, about a mile from Lenox, Massachusetts. Henry Hadley, in 1934, had given what were called starlight concerts there. The concerts were sponsored by the Berkshire Festival Association, headed by Gertrude Robinson Smith, a local power. The performances, given under large tents, were of such a nature that it was felt an annual reenactment of them was in order. The orchestra was invited to be the performing orchestra in the projected series. Thus, when we were informed that we were expected to play a week's concerts in Lenox, there was little or nothing some of us could do, least of all myself, a new member. Still, it was only for a week!

First players, accustomed to returning to their homes in Europe for the summer, did not like the idea of returning to America for one week of concerts. Thus arose an opportunity for second players to fill the positions of their vacating leaders. Foremost among those absent for one reason or another was Georges Laurent, first flute. His reason for remaining in France was legitimate—he had just undergone an operation for a hernia. He sent in his place Marcel Moyse, the reigning flutist of France in that period.

But Moyse found himself in difficulties. His flute was tuned to a 440 pitch. We played at 444, at moments somewhat higher depending on the solo players of the orchestra. Moyse's attempts to reach the higher pitch were disastrous. And he was a stubborn man! When offered a brand new Powell flute, built to our higher pitch, he questioned the donor with "Americain?" and handed the flute back without blowing even one note.

The week's concerts were very successful, the second players covering themselves with glory obvious to all. Never again during the following years was a first player absent!

With our acceptance as the orchestra that should play the concerts planned by the Berkshire Festival Association, it became apparent that something should be done in the way of making available suitable locations for housing and other needs of the players. But first and foremost, attention was given to the needs of the conductor. Ernest B. Dane was our president of trustees in those years. A very wealthy man, Mr. Dane customarily wrote a check for the deficit incurred each year by the orchestra, an amount commonly spoken of as being $150,000. He was a generous man.

At one moment, meeting Gregor Piatigorsky on a street in London, he questioned why Piatigorsky seemed so downcast. The answer came that he had just visited W. E. Hill's and played on a marvelous Montagnana cello, which he could not afford to buy. Dane simply proceeded to Hills's, bought the instrument, and presented it to Piatigorsky.

Dane took the problem of Koussevitzky's residence very seriously. In those years, there were estates in or around Lenox on which taxes had not been paid; the town was simply holding them until the taxes should be paid by whomever. An estate high on the hill overlooking the area caught Dane's eye. Learning that Koussevitzky could be satisfied with a residence in such a commanding area, Dane paid the taxes and made a gift to the conductor. I believe nearly one hundred acres with all necessary buildings was included, the house itself furnished with paintings, silver, and necessities. Though I cannot speak with authority, the price quoted by those who said they knew totaled $18,000. The estate's name quickly became Seranak, a combination made up of the names of Koussevitzky and his wife, Natalie. Natalie was not to outlive those years by any long period.

In 1937, during a concert held at Holmwood under a tent, a frightful storm interrupted our playing. It was necessary to start over, but we were again interrupted by torrents of water that ran down the ridge-poles of the tent under which orchestra and audience were housed. Accompanying thunder made it impossible for the music to be heard. Koussevitzky turned to our audience and announced that this condition could not be allowed to continue. "Ve must haf a hall or shed for our concerts!" Behold, an amount was almost immediately raised, a famous designer and architect were engaged, and the next summer we had such a shed. Built with a double roof for acoustic reasons, it was intended that never again should the concerts be interrupted by any storm that might sweep the area. The wished-for result was reached and has shown its efficacy many times since.

The new shed was erected permanently during the spring and summer of 1937 on an estate presented by Mrs. Gorham Brooks of the Tappan family. I understood at the time, the estate became the property of the Boston Symphony Orchestra "so long as it should be the performing orchestra at the Berkshire Festival." I cannot verify this assertion. The estate had a long history, which included residence of Nathaniel Hawthorne and several others. Hawthorne's *Tanglewood Tales* had been written there. The festival itself came to be known as Tanglewood, though the proper name should be Berkshire Symphonic Festival.

Tanglewood now became an obsession with Koussevitzky, possibly erasing from his mind the recent disappointment at not having returned to Russia with "his" orchestra. We began to hear it spoken of very frequently as we rehearsed in Symphony Hall. Occasionally, he would mention that he had been giving advice on its development. Remarking that some had told him that we should pattern its development after that of Salzberg in Austria, he stated, "Ve vill create our own Salzberg in Tonglevood."

I have mentioned Koussevitzky's difficulties in indicating the irregular meters that were beginning to be the regular fare found in newer works. His elongation of unevenly notated measures had to cause near disaster on more than one occasion, but when only the orchestra was performing, the players managed to conceal his discrepancy, and we learned how it must be done. But with a soloist, the result might be a bit different. We had performed the new Prokofieff's Violin Concerto no. 2 several years before with Heifetz and had managed to hold together even to the point of recording the work for RCA. But we had not the familiarity with this concerto that could allow us to relax in its performance. We performed it on a Friday afternoon and again on a Saturday evening. The Friday performance had gone moderately well, the players remembering what to do with the third or last movement, when the playing gets really rough. But this Saturday evening's performance was not to be as smooth as had been Friday's. At midpoint in the last movement, we found ourselves without clear directions from the conductor. Heifetz was playing as impeccably as always, insisting on his part's being given its proper rhythmic due.

The violin is accompanied, more or less, by a prominent bass drum figure at this point. We fastened on this bass drum figure and accompanied the soloist in spite of what the conductor might be doing with his baton. The concerto reached its conclusion and conductor and soloist left the stage together. Heifetz returned alone. Koussevitzky had immediately dashed up the back stage stairs to his room and refused to heed the call from Heifetz, "Serge Alexandrovitch, come down!" Heifetz was forced to accept the applause alone.

But it would be unfair to imply that his baton technique was completely inadequate. Only in the highly complicated latest works did his failings show up. In others he stood alone.

Shortly after I joined the orchestra, our solo contrabassist, Max Kunze, passed away. It was announced that auditions would be held in Tanglewood during the coming summer to fill the position. All were invited to listen, but the judging of candidates would be in the hands of Koussevitzky and solo players of the orchestra.

At the proper time, we listened to those desiring the position, for the players of the orchestra were there in a body, some simply out of curiosity. It quickly became evident that a certain player was the superior player in all aspects. Ballots were distributed to the solo players for them to indicate their choices and then given to Koussevitzky, who placed them in his pocket as he collected them. He informed us that he would tell us the result of the voting next day.

To our astonishment, no mention was made of the finer player, but the position was given to another! No one among the solo players could be found who had voted for the new first bass. All had voted for the same player, he who had been denied the position.

Our traveling to the "provinces," as Koussevitzky called them, or even to the larger cities on our schedule, was done in the best of style. A special train usually of five cars was ours to use. It consisted of at least one baggage car, two cars for the players, a diner very often, and one other for the use of Koussevitzky alone.

No one else was supposed to use his car unless invited to do so. Often his invited guests might include Georges Mager, first trumpet; Willem Valkenier, first horn; Victor Polatschek, first clarinet; and perhaps George Judd, our manager. That would be it.

In my first season, while enjoying my meal in the diner, I was informed by Leslie Rogers, our librarian, that Koussevitzky wished to see me. When I reached the car that was looked on as too holy for the rest of us, I found him with Mr. Judd, Mager, and Valkenier. Their dinners had been served in his car. As I presented myself, Koussevitzky looked at me and said, "Humphrey, vot nationality you are?"

"Scotch, Irish, Welsh, and some German," was my reply.

"You see?" This to George Judd. "Thonk you."

I never knew what had inspired his question, and I never had any other occasion to pursue the subject.

There were times when the maestro might be forced to violate his own laws of privacy. Occasionally, we might find him waiting in one station or another for the train that was to pull us onward in our journey, when we might be riding special cars on a regular train. At such times he seemed to enjoy the camaraderie that such moments allowed and appeared to enjoy the chats with one or another member of the orchestra who might have worked up enough courage to approach him.

I recall a meeting in the Terrace Station in Buffalo. The orchestra was usually instructed to board our train there, since it was not too far away from our hotels and much more easily reached than the main station in town. We were all huddled into this small room, Koussevitzky in his great coat, simply one among a group of one hundred of more.

Smiling at some conversation of the moment, he was startled, as were we all, to hear the famous bassoon solo that begins the Stravinsky *Le sacre du printemps* sounding out in the liquid tones of a Woolworth ten-cent store fife. So incongruous that it was impossible not to laugh, we burst into applause at its conclusion. Of course, the perpetrator of this moment of music and humor was none other than Jesus Maria Sanroma, the orchestra pianist.

Chu-chu, in addition to his phenomenal powers as a pianist, was also an incorrigible prankster who carried with him certain props that might allow him to create moments of humor such as this.

Of course, I formed friendships with players as time passed. The warmest was with Charles Van Wynbergen, a violist who had come to the orchestra as early as 1910. At that time, it was composed entirely of German players, and some of the tales he was able to tell were ludicrous in the extreme. One still stays with me.

Charlie was an inveterate fisherman. Give him a pole and string with bent pin attached, and Charlie would fish even in a pan of water. So he was the perfect patsy for an escapade that involved him and about five others. In 1916, Charlie was invited to go fishing in Boston Harbor. At the agreed-upon time, the group met and a long skiff was rented for the fishing expedition. Charlie came with all his fishing paraphernalia. Strangely, the only equipment the others had thought to provide consisted of a keg of beer. Charlie was elected to row.

After what he thought was far enough he complained that he was growing tired, whereupon one of the group said, "All right, we have gone far enough. I know these waters and over there is a perfect spot for fishing, and we can tie up to that buoy." A rope attached them to the buoy, and Charlie set himself up for his favorite sport. The others knocked the bung out of the keg, and soon the beer was flowing to their satisfaction.

Hardly had they tied to the buoy before they were conscious that a boat was coming in their direction, throwing bow waves of considerable dimensions in its haste to reach them. About a hundred feet from where they were moored, the boat drew up, and a chap with a megaphone called, "What the hell are you doing out here?" "Fishing," Charlie replied. "Do you know what you are tied up to? You're tied up to a floating mine!" Horrified, Charlie did not dare to row back to the buoy and untie the mooring rope. He simply cut the line and, as quickly as he could, rowed from the vicinity. Whereupon the Coast Guard cutter, for such it was, came alongside their little boat and the questioning began in earnest. "Who are you, and what are your names?"

"Van Wynbergen, Theodorowicz, Kraft, Augnesi, Ludwig, Mann," came the answers. Whereupon the Coast Guard rounded them all up and saw them put in a cell downtown. There was a concert that night, so it was necessary for the manager, Mr. Brennan, to appear at the jail and stand good for the group of players who had inadvertently brought themselves under suspicion of being enemy aliens. With those names, it was not at all difficult to understand the action of the Coast Guardsmen. How were players to know that in that year Boston Harbor had been mined to protect it against all intruding vessels or U-boats?

Charlie sat on the third stand of the viola section. With our forming a friendship, he divulged to me that he was intending to return to his native Holland. With each year, his intention seemed to grow stronger. But I had been in the orchestra eighteen years before Charlie retired, and even after that he continued to work in the library. By that time I realized that Charlie's intention was more to be thought of than actually to occur, and I had been lucky to realize it and not wait for it to happen. By the time it happened, I had moved quite far ahead, and Charlie had been pushed back in the section.

Guest appearances were few among conductors, for Koussevitzky was a hard worker, and the time had not yet come when a so-called permanent conductor is only permanent for a few weeks at a time before he takes himself to another orchestra to exhibit his bag of tricks before returning to his permanent post for a few more weeks. It is far easier for a conductor if he does not have to prepare thirty weeks of programs, as Koussevitzky did, since he can subsist on a certain number of performances that he has already prepared.

In 1937, Serge Prokofieff appeared with us. He had previously been to Boston in 1931 as composer, soloist, and conductor. His programs were not well received, the audience sitting on its hands, as it were, no doubt due to the nature of his newest compositions that he had brought with him at that time. He had been much incensed at the treatment he felt he had received at the hands of the Boston audience.

Interviewed upon his arrival at South Station, he remarked that he still felt the insult, but that this time he was bringing music down to the level of the Boston listeners. "I have brought my first concerto, my first symphony, and a piece I have written for children to listen to." One might have supposed that his coming audience would be aware of the insults he was attempting to throw their way.

True to his word, he played his first symphony, his first concerto, and as a clincher, a piece he called, *Peter and the Wolf*. Again he was composer, soloist, and conductor.

Peter is introduced by a narrator who begins, "My dear children." Imagine! To an audience of Friday afternoon ladies! He goes on to explain that each character of the tale is represented by a corresponding instrument of the orchestra. The work abounds in difficult passagework for each of the solo players of the woodwinds.

Prokofieff was of a rather nasty temperament. At one point in his first rehearsal, he was told by Victor Polatschek that what he had written for the clarinet was impossible. That instrument is supposed to describe the climbing of the cat into the tree. Prokofieff answered Polatschek, "It can be played, it has been played, and it will be played," intimating that if Victor could not do it, someone would be found who could. Polatschek had always played an instrument that incorporated the older system of key arrangement. He had never felt it necessary to switch to the more modern key arrangement of the Boehm system. His technique was astounding, thus his ability to do anything written up to then on his older clarinet and its system.

Challenged by Prokofieff's remark, Polatschek set himself to the task of making the older instrument do the work of the newer! He conquered it admirably and was to play the passage many times with considerable distinction thereafter when it had become an important part of our repertoire.

The very first performance was given with Richard Hale as narrator. He strode to the center of the stage, announced, "My dear children," and the performance went its way. Polatschek's cat climbed into the tree with alacrity. At the end, the audience gave Prokofieff a hearty warm applause instead of the coldness that they might have given in reply to his earlier statement as to their ability to understand his music. The piece was to become extremely popular, and we were to play it many, many times under the baton of Koussevitzky.

Some years later, in Tanglewood, Eleanor Roosevelt appeared with us to recite the same piece as though she were speaking to her grandchildren. The concert was very successful. The following week we were scheduled to record it with her as narrator.

Shortly after her opening statement, "My dear children," as she continued her narration accompanying our music, Koussevitzky, taking the opportunity while the recording company, RCA, was changing waxes or tapes, as the case might have been, looked down at Richard Burgin and asked, "Richard, vot language she speak?" To him, her English was not recognizable. Small wonder!

We gave the very first performance of Copland's *Lincoln Portrait*. Will Geer was the featured narrator, and he gave to his words the nasal twang Lincoln is said to have had. Not always intelligible to Koussevitzky, however, we got some very ludicrous pronunciations of the very American phrases Copland had employed.

While rehearsing a work of Benjamin Britten, the cow horn was being played by Roger Voisin, one of the trumpeters of the section. Upon hearing Voisin's playing of this weird instrument, Koussevitzky remarked, "Voisin, dot is the first time I haf heard a cow with a vibrato." Such a remark allowed laughter from the players, of course.

Nikolai Berezowsky was scheduled as guest conductor, his program to include one of his own symphonies. An accomplished conductor as well as a fine violinist and composer, he stood before us, at work on his symphony. Koussevitzky occupied his usual seat in first balcony right during the rehearsal. Starting the scherzo of the symphony, Berezowsky encountered difficulties. Nothing he seemed to do seemed sufficient to get us off to a good start. After several times, we heard, "Nikolai, I vill show you how to begin the movement." Down to the stage came Koussevitzky. He ascended the podium, raised his baton, and with a gesture or two, we started in perfect ensemble.

Berezowsky could not fail to see what Koussevitzky had done, but nevertheless frowned on the idea of doing it himself. We were normally treated to several preliminary beats when embarking on a scherzo movement that demanded precision.

Koussevitzky, in listening to Berezowsky's music, had determined that his scherzo was written in phrases of three and, in starting us, had given three preparatory beats that gave us his tempo immediately, much as he usually did in the scherzo movement of Beethoven's *Eroica*.

Natalia, Koussevitzky's wife, very often attended our rehearsals. She would sit in a position to the right of the stage, generally in the first balcony. She had a benign expression, was given to no remarks. We grew used to her presence, knew that she meant no harm to anyone. She would move to Koussevitzky's room during intermission of the rehearsal and sit in a corner. Just being there seemed sufficient.

There she was one day when Pierre Luboshutz came running in to see her husband. Luboshutz and Koussevitzky were very old friends, Pierre having been accompanist to Koussevitzky as far back as their Russian days together when Koussevitzky toured as a bass soloist.

Luboshutz exclaimed, "Serge, you are the world's greatest conductor."

"You are very kind, but you must be mistaken."

"No. I say it again. You are the world's greatest conductor."

"Surely there must be another great conductor."

"All right, name one."

Challenged thusly, Koussevitzky turned to Natalia over in the corner and queried, "Natalia, who?"

The story was circulated that during his holding court after an exciting concert, a staunch admirer had remarked to him, "Doctor, I have been wondering for a long time how I should describe you, and today I decided you are a god!"

Came the reply, "Thonk you. You see, I haf my responsibilities."

The story went the rounds. Many wondered at its truth. One, Georges Mager, our first trumpet, decided he must know the truth of the matter. In their next meeting, he told Koussevitzky the story and asked if such an incident had really happened. Koussevitzky, after a moment or so, replied, "It sound like me."

It was Koussevitzky's custom to invite "friends" to hear our final rehearsal on Thursday morning. As many as forty such friends were sometimes in attendance. We grew to think of those Thursday rehearsals as "vaudeville days," for Koussevitzky seemed given to showing his power over the players during those three hours. All sorts of foolish remarks were made.

I recall one morning when a goodly number of Catholic sisters were in attendance, perhaps ten or so. Suddenly, we received a blast that informed us that "I know vot is the matter. You do not believe in God." Although this was directed toward the bass section, it was meant for all of us, we knew.

Jesus Maria Sanroma, our official symphony pianist, was already a member of the Harvard Musical Association, a society given over to providing a series of chamber music concerts as part of its musical activity, with artists of the caliber of Emanuel Feuermann, Isaac Stern, Benno Rabinoff, and Lee Pattison. Any of these appeared only once per season, however.

Sanroma had the hope that players of distinction could be added to the HMA, players who could be expected to take part in chamber music concerts within their own organization. He queried several of us as to our willingness to join the HMA and found us willing. So he sponsored Rolland Tapley as violinist, myself as violist, and Karl Zeise as cellist. For the fourth member, for second violin,

Malcolm Holmes of Harvard University was invited to join. At the same time, in 1940 or thereabouts, we became members of this august organization.

Almost immediately, Sanroma saw an opportunity for us to perform with him during a so-called members' night program. He would be the master of ceremonies and the pianist at the same time. We chose, for that first time, Dvořák's Piano Quintet in A Major. There was an immediate recognition among all of us that the ensemble was a most fortunate one, and we grew very interested in its future.

Very shortly, we were offered an opportunity to appear at the Flute Players' Club, an organization given over to concerts of chamber music groups and to music of a newer nature. We obviously needed another work for that concert. We discovered Dmitri Shostakovich's Quintet for the same grouping. We did not like it at first reading, recognizing its very close affinity to his Fifth Symphony. We intended to return it to the Boston Music Company since we had only taken it out on trial. But since we were rather forced to find a new composition for the concert at the Flute Players' Club, we thought we had better give it another chance.

A series of rehearsals that totaled twenty-five occupied us for some weeks, after which we performed it at the Flute Players'. As we rehearsed, we found ourselves growing rather fond of the work. It was completely Russian in content and spirit, a work that would have been given certain treatment by Koussevitzky had it been designed for orchestra.

Sometime in our early consideration of its contents, we had all agreed that we would prepare this music in "our own way," not the way Koussevitzky might do it, for we recognized his habit of stretching or compressing the music he touched because "I like it dot vay."

We performed the concert at the Flute Players' as the Berkshire Quartet with Sanroma, not knowing that the Berkshire Quartet already existed, though in name only, no concerts having been given by it for quite a few years. We were very soon informed, almost within hours, that we had usurped the name of a noble group. So we were unable to continue under the name we had used.

But other factors were at work. Elizabeth Sprague Coolidge was well known to Malcolm Holmes. Yearly she commissioned new works and gave bronze medals to those who she felt had done outstanding work. She asked us to perform the new Shostakovitch work and had specified that we perform it in Coolidge Auditorium located in the Library of Congress. Since we thought it might appear a good thing to perform it for Koussevitzky before our Washington appearance, we asked him if we might play it for him. He was delighted. Natalia, his wife, had passed away in January of 1942, and Koussevitzky was living alone on Goddard Avenue with only his valet.

He seemed to be very pleased that we were coming to play for him. But knowing of his great liking for honey, I sent to Fayetteville, New York, and secured a ten-pound bucket of unrefined clover honey. When he appeared at his door, we made a present of it to him. He immediately called for a spoon and took a large amount of it, exclaiming that "I eat it like soup."

The playing went well, drawing from him the statement that "You blay it like I had taught you," the exact opposite of what we had striven to accomplish. In the conversation that followed, he asked what name had been chosen for the new group. We explained that we were momentarily without a name. He informed us that "You are the Tonglevood Quartet!" Since the name, "Tanglewood," was almost synonymous with his dreams of the moment, we could find no reason to argue with him, and we knew that no one was likely to ever interfere with our use of the name.

The Boston Symphony was shortly to give the Russian Relief Concert in Washington's Constitutional Hall. Our invitation by Mrs. Coolidge was for a date the following night. When Koussevitzky learned that we were to give a first performance of the new Shostakovich Quintet, he told us we should stay over in Washington and let the orchestra go on to New York without us. He went even one step further. He got in touch with his old friend, Maxim Litvinoff, the Russian ambassador residing at the Soviet Embassy, and suggested our group give a very special hearing to the Litvinoffs and their invited guests, the guest list to be made up from the membership of the Supreme Court and their wives.

The relief concert was wildly applauded. The next morning we presented ourselves at the Soviet Embassy and were shown to our rooms upstairs. In a few moments, we were informed that our audience was in readiness for our performance. Koussevitzky had elected to remain in Washington for this very unusual event. As we took our places and tuned our instruments, a little lady next to him remarked, "Wasn't that a splendid concert last night?" As Koussevitzky drew himself up in the most proper manner to accept her congratulations, she went on, "Were you there?" I can think of no better way to deflate an ego.

So that evening we were appearing in Coolidge Auditorium at the Library of Congress. I was quite aware that in Washington was resident the most famous group of that time, the Budapest Quartet, there under the aegis of Gertrude Whittall, she who had presented the library with a fabulous quartet of Stradivari instruments as well as one or two others, with bows for playing them, Tourtes and others, of an excellence to match the instruments. I could not conceive of their wishing to attend our concert for there was no comparison between our performance and theirs, and an appearance in their midst could be considered presumptuous if they chose to view it as such.

We took our places. The hall was crowded to its last seat, except for four seats in the first row of the auditorium. The lights went down as we finished our tuning. I breathed a sigh of relief when I saw no face of the quartet membership. But I breathed too soon, for with the lowering of the lights, the rear door opened, and four men made their entrances straight down the middle aisle and to the very front row, to those very four seats. No doubt about it, here were the men I most dreaded to see!

I looked across to Rolland Tapley and whispered, "The Budapest Quartet." Tapley gave them a quick glance and remarked benignly, "Good for them." After the concert, they were gracious enough to come backstage to congratulate us on our performance, examine our instruments, look at the parts of the quintet, and in every way show a friendliness we had not expected.

That night we took the B&O train, leaving at one o'clock, for the return journey to New York, where we would rejoin the orchestra. As we found our berths in the train, we were perhaps not too quiet. Three of us had lower berths, the other two uppers. In between their berths, another occupant was obviously asleep, we thought. Karl Zeise chose the upper because there was more room to store his cello. He placed it in its best location for riding through the night, then set himself to the task of retiring. We were a little bit noisy. Suddenly, the occupant of the middle upper berth rose up and exclaimed, "Ah, a cello. Where are you fellows from?"

"Boston," came the reply.

"Do you know Malcolm Holmes?"

"Present," called Malcolm from one of the lowers. Our new friend turned out to be Peter Swing, son of the then very well-known Raymond Gram Swing, radio commentator. In the morning, we all made our way across on the ferry from New Jersey to New York, continuing our friendship. Such was my meeting with Peter and a friendship that has continued through these many years. He was to spend much time in Tanglewood during ensuing summers.

Koussevitzky was not loved by the personnel. They feared his remarks, musical or otherwise, and avoided all but the most necessary contacts. Of course, there were exceptions to this generally held feeling, several players who could not be intimidated. At one point, Koussevitzky questioned a certain violinist, "Mr. L—, are you playing every note?" Mr. L. simply answered, "Seventy-five dollars worth," that amount being the weekly paycheck he received.

During a rehearsal of one of Aaron Copland's new works, there was a bit of confusion in the woodwind section. Copland sat above us in the second balcony. When he interjected a remark that implied that the piccolo player was miscounting, Koussevitzky replied to him, "He do not miscount. His part must be wrong." It turned out that this was exactly the case, and the piccolo player was exonerated. Another instance of the conductor's defending his players' abilities.

As I sat in the orchestra during those early years, I could not fail to be inoculated with the spirit that seemed to permeate the body of players under Koussevitzky's command. They seemed to hate every gesture, every word, and each player seemed to have his own special phrase to express his personal feelings or wishes. One was often heard to remark in a Scottish accent, "I hope I can outlast the blooming bloody blighter!" I still had a lot to learn, of course.

I saw, as all the others did, that his treatment of certain players could not be considered fair or kindly. I stored such incidents in my mind for future consideration. To me, he had been a savior at a time when I really needed the rescue he provided. But with the passage of time, I began to observe that his criticisms were directed toward instruments of the orchestra and not at their players. Only occasionally would he call by name the player who was responsible for the sound he felt should come from the instrument named. Certainly, he expected nothing but the heavenly sounds he heard in his head, and to receive less infuriated him.

He had been a dictator of a sort, for in 1929, the year of his arrival, he had been given a free hand to make of the group he was to lead "de graitest orchestra de I can create." With his second year in command, the personnel of players saw many new faces, not less than a few coming from Paris, young men who were expected to give new life to this already old and famous organization. To him, it was too old, too German, and in need of many changes. He provided for these changes and thereby gained his reputation for cruelty. Perhaps he felt the end justified the means.

Yet I recognized that there are many fine players who do not give of their best unless they hear the flick of the whip of authority near their ears. Then they give of all they have. The orchestra was continually at a nervous tension that caused it to play better than it could, if one may be forgiven for stating what seems to be an impossibility. But it was so. I found myself playing in a way I had not realized was possible, and undoubtedly, this was the effect on many another player. The concerts were the easiest part of the work, the rehearsals something else again.

At no time did the players wish to be singled out for his special attention. Customarily, it is the habit of orchestra players to do a little woodshedding on their instruments as they wait for the moment to go on stage for either rehearsals or concerts. They usually sit around backstage during this last-minute activity. But not when Koussevitzky was on hand. The side of the stage from which he entered would be totally deserted. Players belonging on that side of the stage were in fear of even trying over a difficult passage for their instruments lest they be heard by the maestro while he awaited his moment of entrance in his room above.

When a reduced orchestra was playing a Mozart symphony, for example, and the rest of us awaited our turn to enter and become a part of the orchestra necessary for the larger work which might follow the Mozart, the sound of applause greeting the performance would be the signal for all to vacate that side of the stage where he would exit. There would be a wholesale scurry to be out of reach. We would move to the other side backstage and await the signal to enter the stage, but now from the left-hand door. Confrontations were to be avoided if at all possible. Even a suggestion of difficulty in passagework involving any instrument, if heard by him, could call down upon us either a personal demonstration by the player or the section facing the difficulty. It was far better to guard against such a request by not playing over anything within earshot of the conductor.

I was the floater in my early years in the orchestra. I had been sitting on the second stand for several weeks because of the sickness of another player. During this time, we came to New York for our regular appearance there. Coming out to take my place, I found another player, from the fifth stand, sitting in *my* place. I reminded him that I must sit there, but he, with great disdain, refused to move. I could do nothing but take his place, for the lights were already dimming. Koussevitzky came to the stage and, after his bows, caught sight of the player who had usurped my place. He stepped down from his position, walked over to the usurper, and ordered him back to his position. He signaled me to take the now-vacated place, and with that I could do nothing but step down and take the place I had been using for some weeks. I felt terribly embarrassed.

Koussevitzky had an uncanny ability to recognize the particular technique of young composers, their idioms. Often he resorted to the use of two young pianists, Arthur Fiedler and Jesus Maria Sanroma, who were required to reproduce, on two pianos, the score of the work at hand. Tonally, this was all they could do, of course, but Koussevitzky was thus enabled to examine the young composer's writing and familiarize himself otherwise with the score to be played.

On one occasion, at least, he discovered a discrepancy which sent him to the trans-Atlantic telephone to confer with Darius Milhaud in Paris. It turned out that Koussevitzky had indeed found the error that existed, and the score and parts were corrected before the performance of the work.

Our concertmaster, Richard Burgin, was an invaluable man in that position. Russian by birth, he not only spoke that language fluently, but had considerable command of German, French and English, this last to a surprising extent. An expert at both bridge and chess, he was known for his ability to use his powers of judgment in a measured manner to find the best solution to a problem that might be plaguing us.

An excellent violinist, a good conductor, he was a marvelous leader of the violin sections with a fine judgment of the best bowings to suit the music being played. The only criticism one might level at him was that his violin tone was one of a wiry nature, due to the use of a very fast vibrato, which he seemed unable to slow down. Yet a very fine concertmaster. He had come to the orchestra during the reign of Monteux and was to remain through the reigns of Koussevitzky and Munch, an expanse covering forty-two years in all. Stupendous! Only a few weeks ago in this year 1977, he came up from Florida and became concertmaster of the local opera performances with Sarah Caldwell. At age eighty-four, he feels that he still has a lot of playing to do!

There was a moment in 1941 when the committee was called in to see Koussevitzky. He had dismissed the bass trombone player the previous year, and the player was asking for still another year during which he might save some three thousand dollars. He had previously refused to play on the Esplanade, preferring to use that time to sail his *Friendship* sloop in the nearby Atlantic waters. We heard the evidence of both sides, then heard Koussevitzky say, "But he is an old man and this is not a benevolent society." Koussevitzky was at the time sixty-seven, the trombonist but fifty-seven. In spite of our wish to give the trombonist another year, we were unsuccessful.

No player is ever beyond criticism, not even the leader of a section. He can be destroyed by a remark coming from the conductor to the point where his future worth to the orchestra becomes little or none. Having seen such incidents before, it is no wonder that the individual player may feel himself singled out for something he knows he didn't do, but could do. The hypnotic eye of the conductor will rob him of the ability to play even the simplest exercise! Players need the constant insistence that they are capable of the task in which they are engaged. Of course, if this assurance is not given them from others; they must make every attempt to convince themselves that they have all the abilities they ever had or need at the moment to do their tasks.

Just before my time, while rehearsing Rimsky-Korsakov's *Russian Easter Overture*, Koussevitzky was so entranced by the playing of the second trombone's solo, which depicts the appearance of the drunken Friar during the festivities of the Easter celebration, that he stopped and said, "Hansotte, dot is the most beautiful I haf ever heard. Please blay again for my pleasure." Hansotte obliged with the first two notes, a major second.

"Ah, yes, Hansotte, but the interval is too wide. Again."

"Ah, now the interval is too narrow. Please again."

Thus it went on until Hansotte had tried seventeen times to please the conductor. Growing more nervous with each attempt, Hansotte was now unable even to locate the mouthpiece, while Koussevitzky became more incensed at each attempt. Finally, he called, "Rogers, remove this man from the stage." Hansotte was removed. He was later to return to his position, but never again would he be able to play with the conviction he had first exhibited.

At one moment, Koussevitzky commanded the bass section, "Blay E flat." It was done.

"Now blay E natural." It followed. The difference was not sufficiently apparent, at which Koussevitzky shouted, "Blay anything. Bah!"

He instructed the wind section: "First you must haf the desire; don you must do it with your mouth!"

One of our newer horn players had made a very bad showing in the "Siegfried Horn Call" in a recent performance. In the tuning room, before our concerts, we were being bombarded by this call from the new horn player. He could negotiate everything but the top high note, which persisted in coming out as something else.

One Saturday evening, he finally reached it. After several tries, it came out as hoped for. Sitting at one of our tables playing cards was Lorbeer, our oldest horn player. He had been a very famous player, who was now playing fourth horn, responsible for the very lowest notes on the instrument. Without laying down his cards, Lorbeer took his horn in one hand, raised the instrument to his lips, and played the very high note that had given the young player so much trouble. Then he put the horn down. We never heard the horn call given again during our tuning moments.

Stopping in midrehearsal one morning, Koussevitzky inquired of a certain wind player, "How long you haf been with me?" Silence.

"Please, how long you haf been with me?"

"F-f-ive years."

"Five years. It seems a lifetime, and someday I vill be happy to say good-bye to you." This accompanied by an appropriate wave of the hand.

We were rehearsing a work by Hindemith that called for five soloists, one of them a cellist. Jean Bedetti, first cellist, was playing his part admirably, as was his custom. He was an indefatigable worker at his instrument and very meticulous in preparation of parts he would be expected to play. He had given this particular solo section his full application in his daily practice. All seemed going well until Koussevitzky cautioned Bedetti that he was out of tune. The passage was repeated, and Koussevitzky again remarked that Bedetti was out of tune, at which Bedetti told him, "I am not out of tune. I do not play out of tune." Koussevitzky replied that "you are out of tune." Bedetti now raised his voice and repeated that he did not play out of tune.

With the further insistence from Koussevitzky that he was indeed out of tune, Bedetti rose from his chair, shouted, "Bah!" and stomped from the stage. Koussevitzky simply indicated to Alfred Zighera that he was to play the part, someone else to move in to fill out the desk, and the rehearsal continued without Bedetti. It was not until about three weeks later Bedetti was asked to return. A scene was enacted on the stage that saw the two personalities embracing each other and exchanging kisses on the cheek. Love had returned!

Much as he was susceptible to flattery, Koussevitzky's failure to properly understand remarks made by others would cause him to bridle and resent the kindest remarks they used. On one occasion, while making the trip back to Europe after his season's work in Boston, he happened to meet, while strolling about the ship, Alfred Zighera, cellist from the first stand of the orchestra. Zighera was making his usual return to his native land, France.

"Nu, Zighera, you are vell?"

"Very well, sir."

"And how did you enjoy our season?"

Zighera had played those two seasons with Koussevitzky. Thinking to say the proper thing, Zighera replied, "It was better than the last season, but not as good as the next," considering that he was saying the nicest thing he could think of, a remark often used in answering such a question.

It was not received as it was intended, and Koussevitzky stiffened and walked away. They were not to speak again in the former friendly manner until two or three years had elapsed. I can't say that Koussevitzky ever fully understood Zighera's remark.

Rehearsals, as I have remarked, were the ordeals that the orchestra dreaded. Then he could stop, and very often did, to dwell on details that he felt should be seen to, or simply to exhort us to give everything he desired. He demanded color to the sounds we made, different sounds to the same notes, depending on where they might be used. The most outstanding instance of a player's ability to do this very thing was heard in the playing of Georges Laurent, first flutist. Laurent had the technique, if playing only one long held note, to change the color of it as the music progressed through changes of key, of harmony, or even of instrumentation. He had an uncanny knack of knowing what was needed. His playing was of the very highest order.

A few of the remarks we might hear:

"Piatti, a coup de fonder." (like lightning).

"It is a quadriptiple canon!"

"Like a policeman, I must vatch if you made a not."

"Die Bassi blay like it is notting hoppen. It is hoppen! Ee disturb."

"Horns, I vould like it to haf the korall dot you haf."

"Take it off de beat—de fermata is only for him, you has to be stopped."

"If we played FF, we played notting hoppen, ve must blay MF."

"Ven vill you haf a leetle artistically feeling?"

"It is too ordinaire sound."

"It is not difficult, such ting it is notting to blay."

"Don't made me nervous. If you continue, I vill haf to send you a bill from my doctor."

"Ee don't go vid de gentlemens viddout scandal! You are intelligent people, cultivated people."

"Don't be lazy for de nooances."

"Eet is heavy from self! Vy ve must made more heavier?"

"Don't made me crescendi auf each not."

"My dear, you keel me! Keel me; it vill be better than to listen to you."

"Tuba, you brief too much. You brief so dat a haf not become quatter."

"Second clarinet, you are not together."

"De gentlemans is not clean."

"Und now is again badder." (Still worse.)

"Not good. I haf the habit to haf from you better."

"If no in tune, our tragedy go to de diablo."

"It was awfully not clean!"

"It is stupid ven de conductor made something, and de orchestra don't respond."

"Ve are not togedder; we haf too much tempis."

"Szulc . . . really you are lazy. I must be a policeman to look from your nooances."

"Do not be so scholastically as possible."

"I don't ask *you* to be so modest from the sound!"

"No one from you is a ordinaire man."

Friendships with members of the orchestra were few and far between. Though he was gracious in any meeting with players, few made the effort to reach him in his own greenroom, knowing full well that even a meeting in friendship might soon resolve itself into a discussion or criticism of the player's inadequacies in a moment passed or even longer gone.

Yet there were those who felt that they had known him long enough to chat with him on occasion. Their positions in the orchestra might seem to entitle them to such moments, or a past history of collaboration in Paris might be the reason. They climbed the stairs to see him. He welcomed those visits; yet if the visits of his friends began to assume the appearance of "gossip fests," and tales of other players reached him through these wagging tongues, he could very quickly turn against the tale-carriers and cause them to fail to visit him in the future. Just before I joined the orchestra, a violist was dismissed, one who presumed just too much on the friendship he thought he had.

Koussevitzky's repertoire seemed almost limitless, in the sense that he played music from any country that seemed to him to have produced works that were important enough to be listened to. He used the Teutonic, French, Russian, English literature as well as music composed in this country. And he did them well, seeming to have insight of a high nature, to fathom the composer's intentions or to see within the structure an opportunity to create beauties that even the composer may not have intended or realized.

Koussevitzky had a very special way of treating the music of Sibelius. With this treatment, one could imagine he felt the cold winds of the North sweeping across the stage of Symphony Hall. I grew accustomed to this treatment and to the feeling that accompanied it. If there was a preference for one work, it was certainly the Second Symphony. He played it almost to the exclusion of the others, although each was given due recognition. He seemed to prefer after the Second, the Fifth, and then the First.

But he was given to arranging Sibelius Festivals, during which we would play practically all of Sibelius's writings. During the early years of my membership, Koussevitzky visited Sibelius many times and conferred with the composer as to the correct tempi, balances, etc., of the works he so much loved. After such conferences, he would tell us what the composer had told him. During rehearsals for the violin concerto with Heifetz, we learned that the soloist had said that the last movement of this work was the first thing that had ever given him real trouble. However, it was soon evident that he had found a way to conquer those difficulties. His performance was impeccable, as always.

Perhaps Koussevitzky's "interpretations" were not always of an authoritative nature, but they were, to say the least, a cause for excitement. Even most composers professed themselves astonished at hearing their own music as he interpreted it, and were certainly given food for thought in their future composing. Koussevitzky often remarked that "other orchestras may play in a negligible way, but ve cannot permit." This attitude kept players on tenterhooks, for they never knew what might be asked of them, either singly or severally. One had to learn the score almost with him so that one could know what was probably expected and avoid the personal treatment that would almost certainly follow if one did not produce what Koussevitzky felt was a necessary treatment of the music being rehearsed.

Composers often cast about for new sounds, and in some instances for new ways of producing different sounds from the instruments of the orchestra. Beating on the edges of string instruments, either with bow or knuckles; scratching with fingernails up and down the backs of the violins, violas, or cellos; the so-called Bartok pizzicato, where the string is pulled away from the fingerboard and allowed to snap back to its proper position after hitting the fingerboard, producing a characteristic percussive effect; singing or speaking certain tones while the player is also producing the normal sounds of the instrument he is playing—all these and probably more are still to come.

It will be easily seen that if a string player is using an instrument made by one of the great masters, worth some thousands of dollars, he shrinks from using that same instrument to produce some of the effects so easily asked for by this composer or that. Naturally, an instrument of lesser value will be substituted for the playing of that particular composition.

If such is done, the instrument will be used during the rest of the concert and this can only result in less beautiful sounds wherever these second instruments are employed. It usually happens that a whole section is instructed to produce these unusual effects; the inclusion of such a work can have the result of changing the sound of a large orchestra and cause even the greatest works to fail to have their usual sheen or tonal beauty. The discoveries made during these compositional trials are seldom of a nature that will improve composition in general or music in particular. As a by-product, instruments are often marked in such a manner as to necessitate touching up by a violin restorer, whose charge is usually somewhere in the area of $50. The player feels that he should not be asked to suffer such an indignity or undergo such an expense.

By the time I was a member of the orchestra for several years, I had began to feel that I belonged, understood a little of its working and problems, and when I was asked to run for membership on its committee, I consented and became elected with little or no trouble.

We were a committee of five whose function was to speak for the players when it was necessary to convey a thought or complaint to the conductor, the manager, or the trustees, this last usually done by the manager, however. Only in special cases was there any real reason to take the time of Mr. Dane and the board of trustees. The orchestra was nonunion and always had been. All agreements for our working conditions and salaries were based on agreements reached between these estimable gentlemen and the players. We literally had higher standards of living conditions and salaries than any orchestra in this country, and perhaps the world.

In all controversies between the players and trustees, Koussevitzky stood on the side of the players and defended our rights staunchly. He reasoned that only from satisfied players could he achieve the results he expected. Conversely, having defended their rights, any player owed him the debt of his finest playing. His guarding of the high standards he had set for himself and his orchestra was religious, and he would not step down from his principles, a quality much to be admired.

Shortly after my election to the committee, we were sent for by the conductor himself. He had become very much incensed at something he had read in the newspaper. It seemed that Frank Sinatra, the crooner, was to appear on a Sunday afternoon at the Hotel Statler.

According to the paper, an orchestra was to accompany him that would be led by Arthur Fiedler and players from the Boston Symphony. Fiedler had made it his practice to hire his former colleagues for appearances he was making at an increasing rate of frequency. This was simply another job. Fiedler had earlier been announced as guest conductor in that very season. Koussevitzky had learned that the players engaged included one or two of the first or solo players of the Symphony and had literally become beside himself with rage. Thus our assistance was demanded.

The situation, as he saw it, was described, and he said, "Who is dis man, Sinatra?" Without waiting for an answer, he went on to say, "You must stop dis from happening. Of course, he is an entertainer. But a young girl is also very entertaining—for a little vile, but not for long. You must stop it." Further remarks let us know that he would cancel the guest appearance of Fiedler, only recently announced. I had the courage to tell him that this committee had no jurisdiction over the working habits of our colleagues and that such responsibility for that rested with either the conductor or the manager.

We immediately went to see Mr. Judd, announced our thoughts on the subject, and left it in his hands. The appearance of Fiedler and Sinatra never took place. Neither did Fiedler appear as guest conductor.

We never knew just when Koussevitzky first met James Caesar Petrillo, the czar of the Musicians' Union. But in that meeting, Petrillo brought up the question that had given him much food for thought—how to get the Boston Symphony Orchestra into the union he controlled. Oh, there were ways, as we were to discover, but at that first meeting, Petrillo did not intend using any but the most obvious and direct means. He asked Koussevitzky about how to do it, and Koussevitzky simply replied that he, Petrillo, should speak to our trustees on the subject.

Petrillo was not aware that Koussevitzky lived by certain rules that he had formulated. He made the statement to us that "I haf a great veakness. I promise my friends anything they ask. But I haf it a great strength also. I do not keep my promises." It was very easy to promise Petrillo that he, Koussevitzky, would speak to our president of trustees, Ernest B. Dane, on the subject.

Petrillo thus waited to hear that the meeting had been arranged; but when a sufficient period had elapsed, and he heard nothing, he wrote a letter to our board of trustees, asking for an appointment to discuss the matter. The letter was received and considered, but when Mr. Dane learned just who Petrillo was, he turned a cold shoulder to the idea of such an appointment. Of course, the subject had not been brought to Dane's attention at all, in keeping with Koussevitzky's rule of living. As far as Mr. Dane seemed to feel, the idea was ludicrous, and he simply informed Petrillo that there would be no appointment since there was nothing to discuss. A very unhappy time for the orchestra was thus set in motion.

At about that moment, Toscanini announced his retirement. Stokowski was already gone from the Philadelphia scene, succeeded by a much younger man, Eugene Ormandy, no challenge at that moment to one who might be considered as the foremost candidate for the position as America's greatest conductor. Koussevitzky no doubt saw this honor within his grasp.

We began to feel Petrillo's influence from within our own membership. Certain younger members were very much of the opinion that the orchestra should be unionized and called for a meeting to discuss the possibility. The trustees were, of course, not allowed to show their wishes, for prevailing law made it an illegal act to do so. But no matter how many showed themselves disinterested in the idea of unionization, these younger players would not let the subject die, and we were constantly besieged by them to call a meeting to discuss certain "new facts." It was inevitable that sides should be taken.

Some of us who had formerly belonged to the Musicians' Union had left it to join the Boston Symphony, and over each of our heads hung a fine of $1,000 if we should try to rejoin the organization we had so cheerfully left.

We had no gripes, actually. Our working conditions were already far better than those in effect in any other orchestra in the country, our salaries higher also. Our agreements with the trustees were made by high-thinking gentlemen and were not apt to be abrogated so far as we could see. I could truthfully see no reason why we should wish to exchange what we already had for what would probably be our way of life should we join the union.

Personally, I had only recently been the recipient of some of the rules that I considered unjust. For instance, although one belonged to the union in one city, one could not move to another for a job that was known to exist without joining the union there, waiting out a period of months or years before being allowed employment in anything like a lucrative, sustaining nature. I had only rather recently searched for employment in New York, Chicago, Detroit, and Cleveland, while already a member of the union in Boston. Doors were closed to me simply because I did not belong to the union in any of those other cities. I felt that once joining the union, one should have the same freedom as a plumber or a carpenter in pursuing employment.

Then there was the necessity to engage in a sympathetic strike to support musicians in another city, who were striking for reasons completely their own. For instance, should the New York Philharmonic players be on strike for personal reasons that might have absolutely no connection with us or with unionization in general, why should we be expected to refuse to give our concerts in Carnegie Hall that might have been contracted for as far back as one year?

Naturally, lines were drawn and sides taken. By and large, our membership was made up of Europeans who understood little or nothing of unionization or of the problems that might arise once we had become union members. But the insistence of the minority for the union brought bewilderment to such members, and I can recall more than one instance where some members voted on both sides of the same question, so bewildered were they. They had simply failed to digest the information, or had been at the last moment filled with advice of the wrong kind.

In the meanwhile, Petrillo had begun to use the devices available to him. We began to find ourselves without electricians to turn on the lights in halls that were on our touring schedule. Trucks began to be unavailable for transportation of our many trunks. Many and devious were the devices available to him, and it was not too difficult to foresee an eventual result that could only be disastrous to our orchestra as an institution. Too, we had learned that Petrillo had managed to make it rather impossible for our recording contracts to be fulfilled. He held the whip hand in this respect, for all other recording groups belonged to his union. One thing added to another made his armament imposing indeed.

Our committee had begun to suspect that one of our very own members was working against our efforts to withstand the unionization being forced on us. Eventually, several of us took the suspected member out for dinner and faced him with the accusation. He did not deny it, so we simply asked him to resign from the committee and join in the open with the other side.

Ernest B. Dane, as I have previously remarked, was a very wealthy man who, when he learned the amount of the yearly deficit incurred by the orchestra, simply wrote a check to cover the amount. The amount that year was about $150,000, for which he had not yet written his check. Unfortunately, Mr. Dane was discovered dead in his bed at about the time we were into the very center of our troubles with Petrillo. His passing could be seen, by anyone who knew, as almost the last straw, and without an Ernest B. Dane, our situation was dire indeed. There was almost literally nothing for the remaining trustees to do but inform us of their economic situation and await further developments, whatever they might be.

Eventually, the altercation simmered down to consideration of the two offending bylaws that dealt with transfer restrictions and sympathetic strikes. We were adamant on those two subjects. Petrillo, as national president of the Musicians' Union, had the power to make or rescind any bylaw in their books. He stood as adamant as we on the other side of the question. As an impasse was reached, the Senate Investigating Committee decided to look into the Petrillo affair. He suddenly found himself in need of public support.

In my position of secretary of the orchestra committee, I suddenly received a telegram from him, acceding to our desires and welcoming us to membership in his union. All fines levied on former members of the union who had gone nonunion were waived, of course. In the course of our meetings with him through the months, we had become sufficiently suspicious to realize that we now needed someone to protect us from our protector.

Accordingly, we engaged the services of Judge Jacob Kaplan, who was widely known as an excellent labor mediator and expert on labor laws. For us he did a magnificent job, giving us the very best advice and seeing us through to the end of our battle with Petrillo. In my position as secretary of our committee, I suddenly found myself with the task of putting down on paper the agreements reached between us, our trustees, and the union.

Suspicious of anything Petrillo might say, we had demanded that all agreements from whichever side must be clearly understood and ratified by all concerned. Thus it was that I actually wrote our first trade agreement. In that first agreement, we retained our autonomy to bargain as we always had. The local union officials were to have nothing to do with it except to sign their names to the finished document and take the oath that they would insist on enforcement of all that had been agreed upon.

That original agreement stated that the offending bylaws were to be removed. They could not be replaced except by the action of two successive union conventions held at least ten months apart. So we joined the American Federation of Musicians on December 10, 1942. The following July, the union convention, at Petrillo's suggestion, renewed the two bylaws that had been removed, and one year later, the convention reaffirmed their action.

There we were—caught!

During our negotiations, our trustees had come to respect Judge Kaplan's knowledge and to admire his decision making. Shortly after our entrance into the union, a vacancy occurring in the board of trustees, and he was invited to join their body. He thus became the first Jewish member. I shall speak of him later in another respect.

Koussevitzky's concerto rehearsal technique was almost invariably of a certain pattern. Several days before the appearance of a soloist, we would read the accompaniment through, at least, certain portions that might give trouble. We rehearsed certain of those portions and gave them more than just a glossing over. Then with the appearance of the soloist, things might begin to happen. It was not always that soloist and conductor saw the concerto in the same way. If Koussevitzky disagreed, he did not hesitate to say what he thought. Item after item along the way would be scrutinized until the end of the concerto was reached. Then, "Now ve blay it again," at which we would turn back to the beginning and replay the entire composition.

The manner in which Koussevitzky rehearsed, the means that he used to draw from his players their utmost skills, may seem to have been cruel and unjust, but the net result was that the orchestra responded in a manner to produce sounds probably never before heard from any orchestra of the world. The intention of Koussevitzky had been to "made it the finest orchestra qui existe," and he succeeded.

We were to play the Rachmaninoff Concerto no. 3 with the composer himself. A fabulous pianist, Rachmaninoff had no problems whatsoever with any passagework in any part of the concerto. Having given it the usual piecemeal treatment, Koussevitzky gave his usual order to us and turned his own score back to its beginning. Rachmaninoff stared at him, reached for the piano lid which he closed, shouted, "Bah!" and walked from the stage. An embarrassing moment or two ensued; then we were told the rehearsal was ended.

There were only several who were not the targets of Koussevitzky's remarks. He was not a really good accompaniment conductor. Richard Burgin was far better. It had to be Koussevitzky's way or not at all, except in the cases of certain soloists. Heifetz, he did not criticize, nor did he attempt to change in any way the playing of Myra Hess. All others were not beyond his remarks. We were preparing to play the Brahms Violin Concerto with Josef Szigeti, who was touted as being the foremost authority on the playing of this and the Beethoven concerto. Very soon after the violinist's entrance, the orchestra sings the main theme, and the solo violin weaves a series of quintuplets about it.

We were soon aware that there was disagreement between soloist and conductor. Koussevitzky remarked, "But my dear, the orchestra has the theme, you are secondary." Of course, he was entirely right. Szegeti answered that he was the soloist, and that the orchestra should follow him. There was some discussion with no one winning the argument. Colors began to be high on both faces, and when it was seen that neither had convinced the other, the moment was allowed to pass.

In the concert that very evening, Szegeti insisted on his way, Koussevitzky on his, and there were a few moments when disaster might have overtaken us. These are the moments when the players in an orchestra must exhibit, in a very subtle way, their ability to bring right out of wrong and save what otherwise might be a calamity. Of course, Szigeti did not appear with us again.

Gaston Elcus was a very fine violinist, who sat on the second stand of the first violin section. His coming to the orchestra had followed several auditions, which he played in Paris. He had been offered the post of concertmaster of the St. Louis Orchestra by Rudolf Ganz; Henry Verbrugghen had agreed to accept him for the position of concertmaster of the Minneapolis Symphony; and Koussevitzky had offered him a position in the violin section of the Boston Symphony.

During the moments when he considered what to do, his wife remarked, "Gaston, you might accept the position in St. Louis or Minneapolis, but if the conductor does not continue to like you, you will be far away from home and friends. In Boston you have already many friends from Paris, and the responsibility is much less when you sit in the section than in the position of concertmaster." So Gaston elected to come to Boston.

Shortly after his arrival, the Liszt *Faust* Symphony was the main work of that week. In the second movement, "Marguerite," there is an episode that calls for four violins to play alone, a solo, and three supporting parts. Elcus's position on the inside of the stand gave him the responsibility for the fourth or lower part of the four. Very conscientious by nature, Elcus had returned to the stage before intermission's end, and he was looking over the part he already knew so well, but wished to do to his own satisfaction.

As he played, immersed in his own thoughts, he became vaguely aware of a presence in the chair beside him. Glancing up, he was surprised to see Koussevitzky there. Of course, he stopped, the seemingly polite thing to do. Whereupon Koussevitzky said to him, "Please, Elcus, do not stop. Continue. For me, you haf a halo."

A remark of that nature could not fail to convince Elcus that he truly had a friend in the conductor, and Boston was indeed the place for him to be. The orchestra returned to the stage, and rehearsal was continued. Eventually, the second movement was reached, and further along, the sequence for the four violins was heard. As they played, Koussevitzky stopped them.

Fixing Elcus with his eye, he cautioned him, "Elcus, you are too loud, you are not togedder, your sonority is not good." He continued with several other critical remarks of a derogatory nature at which he was so adept. Waiting until the conductor had finished, Elcus assumed that childlike expression that he could so well put on and asked, "And not out of tune?" This last was the only criticism Koussevitzky had failed to make. But from that time to the end of his stay in the orchestra, Elcus did not presume on his earlier acquaintance with his old friend.

One morning, Koussevitzky announced, "Adam, I vould like it to hear you blay," this to Eugene Adam, who presided over several of the brass instruments, although his customary position was as a member of the trombone section.

The next day, at the proper moment, Adam began transporting the several ponderous instruments from where he kept them in the basement of the Hall to Koussevitzky's room, two flights up. When all was in readiness, the audition was heard by the conductor. Evidently, it was satisfactory, for Adam continued with the orchestra. He was later questioned by Charlie Van Wynbergen, a violist and close friend, as to how it went. Adam answered that it had gone well. Since his audition was done on a set of varied instruments, Charlie was very curious, eventually asking Adam, "Did you play the tuba too?"

"Oh, yes."

"What did you play on it?"

"I played the whole repertoire."

"How long did that take you?"

"Two minutes."

During a rehearsal of Strauss's *Don Juan*, a passage involving the cello section bothered Koussevitzky. Each stand had to play alone; Koussevitzky eventually decided that the fourth stand was at fault. The two players involved were asked to play alone, but their performance was not pleasing to him. With a sarcastic look on his face, he let them know he would hear them the next day. Each of these players was thoroughly capable of negotiating the passage, but under those conditions found their nerves causing a tightness of muscles, which made the task doubly difficult. They spent sleepless hours that night.

The next day, when reaching this same difficult spot, Koussevitzky reminded them of his promise and, in a moment or two, had annihilated any self-confidence they might have built up during the sleepless night they had endured. At the repetition of the fiasco of the day before, we heard, "I vill hear you again tomorrow, and if it is not bedder, I vill send you to the conservatoire." With this, immediately after the rehearsal's finish, Jean Bedetti, our first cellist, took the two cellists with him into one of the empty rooms of Symphony Hall. He heard them play the passage as well as it probably could be played. When he had heard them to his satisfaction, he immediately went to Koussevitzky, still in the hall, reported what he had heard, and intimated that Koussevitzky should "lay off" with the crucifixion. We never heard another word about the passage; the cello section performed to the satisfaction of Koussevitzky in that week's concerts.

I had been in the orchestra five seasons, always waiting for the advancement that I understood was to be mine. During my second season, a violist on the last stand had suddenly died, and since I was the thirteenth violist, it was natural that I should take his place. But there I still sat.

One morning, as we left the rehearsal stage, Koussevitzky said to me, "Humphrey, I vould like to hear you blay, for your career." I had not the slightest idea of what he had in mind, but prepared myself during the next few days. The session was held in Koussevitzky's private greenroom, where I was accompanied by my friend, Jesus Maria Sanroma, the pianist of the orchestra. The Brahms E-flat Sonata was our vehicle, and it was played with most of what I call my ability, although my playing under such conditions has never really pleased me. It seemed, however, to please Koussevitzky. I was dismissed with a pleasant "thonk you."

Imagine my utter surprise when a short time later, I found not one but two new violists joining our section. They were both seated ahead of me! I could not accept such a treatment without asking the reasons why. So I went to Koussevitzky and asked him if I had offended him in a musical way, one in which I could make amends. He greeted me cordially, but to my question, he replied that he had nothing to tell me. He walked away! I followed him and with a slight touch on his shoulder caused him to swing about and face me. I reminded him of his earlier promise and again asked what I had done, to which he replied, "Humphrey, I luf you, but it must be this vay, and I cannot tell you vy." That is all I ever got from him. The reasons for the treatment were long in coming, but I was eventually to discover them.

During those years, which were my first, I had to become conscious of his preoccupation with what "the others were doing." He only spoke this phrase in connection with the two then-foremost conductors of America, Stokowski and Toscanini. He was very conscious of their work with the Philadelphia and New York orchestras, feeling perhaps that these two groups were the only real competition to his Boston group.

As the years unfolded, and the career of Dmitri Shostakovich became an important part of any orchestra's consideration, it was often a neck-and-neck race between the three involved as to who should give first performances of this composer's work. I recall that in one instance, we won by finishing the performance of one of his symphonies five minutes ahead of Stokowski in Philadelphia. It now seems ridiculous, but in those days, this competition appeared important to both of them. Occasionally, Toscanini might grab the honor of a first performance, but he had only entered the competition at a later date, no really serious effort seeming to be made. It just happened.

We had played Aaron Copland's *En salon Mexico* quite a few times, then had laid it aside for a period. But the moment came when it was programmed again, and we took it up for a general look through. At a particular moment, the E-flat clarinet was intoning a very catchy tune, one very rhythmic in character. From somewhere in the wind section came the beating of feet in exact rhythm with the clarinet. In a moment, Koussevitzky became furious and, in his anger, picked up the score and flung it at one of the wind players, shouting, "Are you crezzy?" The score failed to negotiate the distance Koussevitzky intended, and it struck Ralph del Sordo, of the second violin section, on the shoulder.

In a moment, it was followed by the conductor's baton, which did reach its intended victim. Then Koussevitzky stomped from the stage. We sat there for about ten minutes until Burgin left his position and went to find Koussevitzky and get an explanation for this outburst.

In a few moments, the back door of the stage opened, and one of our players was requested to see Koussevitzky. He left the stage, and in a few moments we were told that rehearsal was over. Nothing more was ever said about the incident. But it did not happen again.

During his career as an orchestral conductor in Paris, Koussevitzky had found the time to create a publishing company that specialized in the printing of new compositions of the large group of new composers then competing for world recognition. His Edition Russe had thus become the publishing house of the new music coming from the pens of Igor Stravinsky, Serge Prokofieff, and Darius Milhaud, to name but a few.

In this respect, he seemed to have a sort of genius for properly evaluating the talent or accomplishments of those whom he admitted to his stable of composers. Of course, this affinity with the newer composers did him no harm; instead it gave him a sort of hold over their production, especially if they listened to his suggestions as to what he felt the public wished or he himself commissioned. The list grew long as time passed.

Prominent among the works he had commissioned was an orchestration of Moussorgsky's *Pictures at an Exhibition* by Maurice Ravel. Complete rights for performance were reserved by Koussevitzky so that none other could perform the work as Ravel had orchestrated it. However, Leopold Stokowski, slightly changing certain instrumentation, had managed to produce his own *Pictures*, suspiciously reflecting the abilities of Lucien Cailliet, a player and arranger and a member of the Philadelphia Orchestra. These slight differences in instrumentation kept this Stokowski attempt from being viewed as plagiaristic.

In this country, Koussevitzky had continued to exercise his powers of selection by designating those whom he thought most representative of what he considered important new music. At the head of the list appeared Aaron Copland, with David Diamond, William Schuman, Howard Hanson and Roy Harris, and literally a host of others that would eventually include Leonard Bernstein. In very few instances was he found to have been less than correct in his estimates.

As we played through, for the first time, these new works from American composers, we were often reminded, "Here is the logical sookcessor (successor) to Beethoven." He gave to each one of them equal opportunity to be heard, to the extent that if the Boston audience did not seem to accept their work as he thought it should, the same work was programmed again within the same season to insist on the audience's having had a chance to hear the true beauties of this "great vork."

One morning while we were in New York, I was called by Sanroma, our pianist, and asked if I would care to go with him to hear a candidate for the Berkshire Music Center. Of course, I wished to do so, and after meeting with Sanroma, we found our way to Steinway's on Fifty-seventh Street, where we met the young candidate, Seymour Lipkin. Seymour played some Chopin for us, and very well, indeed. For some reason, there was much confusion at Steinway's, and Sanroma decided to continue the audition at Carnegie Hall. There, in the conductor's room, Sanroma asked Lipkin, "And how do you read?" To Lipkin's, "Pretty good, I think," Sanroma opened the piano part of the Shostakovich piano quintet, turned it upside down, and said, "Let's hear some of this." Lipkin could indeed read very well and acquitted himself admirably. Sanroma had been very sure that Lipkin could not have known the music he placed before him!

We were scheduled to play in Kleinhans Auditorium in Buffalo. When concert time was upon us, an announcement was made that Koussevitzky could not conduct because of illness. Burgin took over the program, and it went well. In the usual order of things, this might have been accepted. But the lady in charge of the concert happened to read in a Rochester paper that Koussevitzky had attended a concert given by the Rochester Philharmonic Orchestra, conducted by Howard Hanson, one in his stable of composers, and their concert had featured a new work by Hanson. The Boston Symphony was not invited back to Buffalo.

With the beginning of the 1944-1945 season, Koussevitzky's twenty-first, we heard him say, "In the past twenty years, we haf accomplished great things! And vot haf the others done? One blay sooper (supper) music (Toscanini), and de other go to Hollywood (Stokowski, for the film *One Hundred Men and a Girl*), so it remains for me to continue de great vork." This time he did not add that some of us would not.

Almost directly ahead of me sat a violist who was given to extravagant movements as he played. We were rehearsing something with an active viola part that demanded quick action from all of us. Somehow, this violist overdid himself, and his bow went flying from his hand. It struck the curtain that always hangs behind the fifth row of seats during rehearsals, this curtain helping to simulate the presence of an audience so far as acoustics are concerned. With a clatter, the bow fell to the floor. Just at that moment, Koussevitzky turned to the viola section for an important phrase it had to play. As we played, the bowless violist mimed the passage, making never a sound. With the end of the passage, Koussevitzky turned again to the violins, never having noticed the lack of bow in the unfortunate violist's hand. With that, our violist made his way over the edge of the stage. We could hear him bumping his head in his search for his bow. He finally found it, miraculously unbroken, and then returned to the spot where he had made his descent to the floor of the hall. No one would assist him for fear of drawing attention to himself. He was forced to go out of the hall, return backstage, and find his way back to his position in our section by crouching down and sneaking in. He heaved a sigh of relief when he completed the maneuver and remarked, "I finally made it."

In 1943, Béla Bartók lay in a hospital bed in New York suffering from a disease that would eventually take his life. Koussevitzky went to his bedside and offered him a commission for a concerto for orchestra. Bartok was renewed, and from that moment, he applied himself to accomplishing the work Koussevitzky had requested.

Eventually, we were to give its first performance. During the rehearsal, Bartók occupied a seat in the first balcony right and occasionally delivered himself a remark or two. At one point, his remarks occupied more time than Koussevitzky's thought proper, so he suggested that they confer during the rehearsal's intermission. The conference was held, Bartók insisting all the way through it that certain things were not to his liking. With the rehearsal's continuance, Koussevitzky announced that the composer was in agreement with all we were doing and ended the report with "And I like it dis vay." The work was to achieve a deserved popularity.

While on tour to Chicago and midwestern points, we traveled in a special train, as was our custom. Following a concert in Ann Arbor, we were scheduled to leave and arrive in Boston early the next day, where, after resting during the day, we were scheduled to give a special concert in the Boston Garden to further the war effort, this being about 1943.

Sometime in the morning of the Ann Arbor appearance, we were informed that we must check into local hotels, remove our belongings from our special train, and be expected to depart from Ann Arbor on a regular train the morning after the concert. This would mean an all-day ride that would put us in Boston for only a short rest before we should be expected to perform in the Garden. There was little any of the players could say, but this did not apply to Koussevitzky. He was thrown into a fury and announced, "I vill call Fronklin." And call Franklin Roosevelt he evidently did, for we were suddenly informed that our special train would be waiting after the concert and leave Ann Arbor at the previously scheduled time.

We were very often the recipients of his thoughts on political affairs. "You vill see, I assure you, stahtues to dis great man in every backyard." He, of course, referred to Roosevelt. And he would, on occasion, advise us how we should vote in a coming election. It was not our custom, however, to be too much swayed by his personal wishes in such matters.

Koussevitzky's concern was with the music we should be expected to produce and realized full well that a concert given after a full day's train ride of six hundred miles would be far below the level of performance he felt should be expected. Whenever there might be a question that involved the traveling conditions, the working conditions in Symphony Hall, or whatever, he always showed himself to be on the side of the players and would argue strongly on their behalf. He sensed that we must have good condition before we could produce the sounds he demanded from us. He never departed from this attitude, certainly a position for which we gave him many thanks and one that helped balance all the items on the other side of the ledger.

In 1945, I received an invitation to join the Chicago Orchestra, certainly one of the leading groups of this country. Never having met the conductor, Désiré Defauw, I insisted on playing an audition for him. I saw the possibility that I might displease him and be asked to resign, for conductors are strange people. We met at the Lotos Club in New York, where I performed everything he asked of me. He wished to talk with me as to conditions in Boston, I learned, and we sat together for a considerable time after the audition. It was agreed that I should leave Boston at the end of the season and join the Chicago group. Hardly had I arrived back in Boston when I learned that Mr. Defauw had been asked to resign. I thanked my stars that I had not gone to the trouble of asking to be released from the Boston Symphony.

To my great surprise, I received an invitation the following year to join the Chicago Orchestra in the same capacity as before, as a player on the second stand with a move up the following year to the first stand. Naturally, I was tempted! I had now been on the last stand of the Boston Symphony for twelve seasons. I had not received the promised promotion. I realized that if ever I was to leave the Boston Symphony, it was fortuitous that I had been invited just at this moment. I would be occupying a position more important than the one I now held, and I would be greeted with a salary already twenty-five dollars per week more than I was making.

I had known Artur Rodziński very slightly before he became conductor of the Chicago forces. I thought that this second invitation might be evidence that the Creator was pointing the way for me, perhaps. I had simply been in Boston long enough. I went to see Mr. Judd, told him I was thinking of leaving, but did not disclose the source of my invitation. Shrewd he was for he said to me, "George, there are only four orchestras that can pay the yearly salary you now receive—Boston, New York, Cleveland, and Philadelphia. Were I to include a fifth, I would say Chicago." I failed to answer his unasked question, however. Then he reminded me that my contract had still a year to run; however, if I could make my peace with Koussevitzky, the trustees would probably waive the agreement between us and let me go, to further the career of a still-young man.

So I approached Koussevitzky, my mind now made up. I explained that I had a good offer from another orchestra and felt that I should accept it. With that, he exclaimed, "But vare you go?"

"I cannot tell you where, but it is a fine large orchestra."

With a shout, accompanied by a beating of the table, he said, "This is de finest!"

"I agree, but there are other people who feel great pride in the orchestras of their cities."

"Humphrey, vy you are unhappy?"

"I have delivered my best from the last stand even though I was promised an advancement when I came into the orchestra."

"Ah, you do not like—." He used the name of a violist who had come into the orchestra several years after me.

"I have no feeling about—."

"So you do not like—?" He named another violist who had also come into the orchestra after my entrance.

"No, I have no feeling about—."

"Humphrey, you are a fine player, and I luf you. Ve vill haf it a competition."

"I do not wish to compete for a position already held by one or another of my friends. I do not need a better position in this orchestra if I take the position I am offered."

"Den ve vill haf a reorganization."

"If I stay here, I must submit to your reorganization, of course."

By this time, the famous veins were standing out on Koussevitzky's forehead, his face blue with anger. I recognized that I had indeed placed myself in jeopardy, and it would be better for me if I simply left without further ado. I found my way out of the room and went to see Mr. Judd. When he learned that I had not parted in friendship with Koussevitzky, he simply informed me that it was not in his power to release me from my contract that ran for another year.

From that time on, I waited for the axe to fall on my head. The power to crucify me with remarks of a derogatory nature were in Koussevitzky's hands, and he had shown himself a great master of the art.

But nothing happened. Weeks passed until I was almost lulled into a sense of security. Too good to last, however. Suddenly, a rehearsal was stopped. Turning to the first violin section, Koussevitzky announced, "Mr. Leibovici, I vould like it to hear you blay this afternoon the first movement of the Brahms Concerto." Leibovici turned grey! "And Mr. Resnikoff, I vould like it to hear you blay the Bach Chaconne today." Resnikoff joined Leibovici in changing color. Then turning to the viola section, he said, "And I vould like it to hear the young boys, Humphrey, Lehner, Bernard, and Cauhape next Monday."

Now l knew the extent of his punishment of me and the cause of the summons to the several of us. It was his way of exhibiting fairness in his treatment of me. It appeared nothing could be done save accede to his request. One player, however, felt differently about it. He went immediately to see Mr. Judd. He told him that although he knew death to be inevitable, he did not wish to know the time and place when his would occur. Eugen Lehner refused to take part in such an audition. Another was insulted that he had not been asked. Kornsand took Lehner's place in the auditions.

I had just been a partner in a coast-to-coast broadcast with E. Power Biggs, the organist. We had also given a recital together within weeks at the Germanic Museum in Cambridge. Fortunately, I thought, a recording of our broadcast had been made, and I had a copy. I saw no real reason why I should have to play an audition.

I offered Koussevitzky, through his secretary, Olga Naumoff, later to become his wife, the recording which he might listen to so that he would know what I could do musically and technically under tense conditions. After a day or so, she returned the recording and told me that Koussevitzky preferred to hear me play. Having nothing else prepared at the moment, I asked Biggs if he would help me out by coming to Symphony Hall and accompanying me on the Symphony Hall organ, an instrument already famous for its excellence. We would again play the work we had used in the broadcast, a difficult piece called "Poeme," written by Leo Sowerby.

On the stage of Symphony Hall stood a full-sized Steinway grand that we were free to use if we wished. Imagine my horror when it was announced that the organ had ceased to function temporarily! Nothing left but to use the Steinway grand! Biggs would play the organ part on the piano, minus, of course, the bass line that was normally played by the feet of the organist.

Koussevitzky had surrounded himself with the concertmaster, the first violist, first clarinetist, and perhaps one or two others whom I cannot name. Lukas Foss sat on one side, on hand to play all the accompaniments required. Somehow, Biggs was able to add enough of the organ part to make the piece sound somewhat like music. My part was unchanged, and I found myself angry enough to have some of my normal command. That has been my usual response when I am either angry or sick in body. I find an extra resource that somehow sees me through. We reached a difficult passage in viola octaves. Koussevitzky stopped us and asked me to play the same passage twice as slow. It had not given me any trouble at its normal speed. Now it gave me less. But now Koussevitzky requested that I play it twice as fast as indicated. That was a horse of another color! However, I managed it somewhere within its intended sound, and we passed on to the remainder of the composition. With the end of the Sowerby "Poeme," Koussevitzky remarked, "Thonk you," and walked from the stage. The listeners were supposed to write their judgments and hand them in to Koussevitzky, at least I supposed they were.

More weeks passed, and nothing had been said. I had given up any idea of going to Chicago, of course. I had been given opportunity to consider the changes that would have to be faced should I make the move. My sons had now sunk their roots into the surroundings I had brought them to instead of letting them grow up in Ohio, my own birthplace and theirs. I had to realize that Ohio was no longer as important to me as it had once been. My relatives were passing from this life as were my friends back home, so I no longer had the same reasons to return for the visits I had tried to make annually.

Then I had to contrast the practical facts of living in Boston rather than in Chicago. In the larger city, I should very possibly have to live quite far out in such a town as Des Plaines or Evanston. I should have to drive into some remote area where I could board the Elevated and travel through the Loop until I had reached a point from which a walk would finally bring me to Orchestra Hall. Should I find it necessary to make the journey twice in one day, I should find myself spending more time traveling than I use for my profession.

In staying in Boston, I needed only twenty minutes for the drive from Arlington to Symphony Hall. I could park my car somewhat near the hall, and not to be disregarded, my drive to work would be by the Memorial Drive and along the beautiful Charles River. I had not fully appreciated the magnificent trees that lined the drive along my route, particularly that section of the drive that lay in the vicinity of Harvard University.

So I wired the Chicago authorities that it was impossible for me to be released from my contract and settled my mind to remain in Boston until another opportunity might present itself. I had not reckoned with other factors, however. During that winter, when I was wrestling with the necessity of making a decision, an incident took place that put an entirely different light on the subject. One of the solo players of the Chicago Orchestra accidentally glimpsed a list of players who were to be dismissed at the end of that very season. His name was among them! Losing no time, he gathered around him all he could remember from a list of thirty-one! They hastened to union headquarters, preferred charges against the conductor for everything they could remember that he had already said or done to them. In short order, he himself was dismissed! I had to wonder if some greater power was looking out for me. When the Boston auditions were behind us, we discovered that the violist who had refused to play had won the audition, in a manner of speaking, for he was moved up to the second stand, displacing others who were moved back. I gained four places, and I would now be playing on the fourth stand.

A longtime player tells this story (Pierre Mayer sat on the first stand of the second violin section within an arm's reach of Koussevitzky):

"I was playing 'ard that morning. Suddenly, Koussevitzky leaned over and said, 'Mayer, you are seeck.' So I play 'arder to show him I am not sick. When intermission came, I ran down to the men's room. I looked at my face in the mirrohr. I looked all right to myself. I had seen my face in the mirrohr when I shaved at home. So when we started to rehearse again, I made sure I played even 'arder. Even if I felt all right, if he thought I was sick, he might ask me to leave the orchestra. But he said to me again, 'Mayer, you are seeck.' So I played still 'arder, but I was very worried. At the end of the rehearsal, I went to see him. (English had thus far been the language used between the two.)

"I say to him, 'Mr. Koussevitzky, you say I am sick, but I feel fine; and you see I play 'ard." (They were now using French for communication.) As Mayer continued to state his great condition of health and asked the question of why he was accused of being sick when he felt as well as he had ever felt in his life, Koussevitzky looked at him in bewilderment, finally stating, "But Mayer, you are not seeck. I am seeck." His pronouns had become confused, of course.

Mayer answered in great relief, "You are sick. Ah, that is bettair!" He headed toward the door, already realizing that he had committed a faux pas, one that would be difficult to explain. As he reached the door, he heard behind him "What you mean, dot is bettaire?" But by that time, Mayer was halfway down the steps and did not stop to argue the case.

During a rehearsal, Koussevitzky pointed to a player in the bass section and accused him of sleeping on the job. The player answered,

"I do not sleep."

"Do not speak and do not sleep."

"I do not sleep."

"You sleep and do not answer me."

"I do not sleep."

"Rogers! Remove this man from the stage."

Without waiting for removal, the player took his instrument and left the stage. Immediately, he rushed up to Mr. Judd's office and announced his resignation. Mr. Judd asked him if it were true that he owned a camp in Scituate. Admitting that Mr. Judd was correctly informed, he heard himself advised to "go fishing" for a few days.

During these several days of "vacation," the committee was summoned by Koussevitzky. We stood before him, and he asked us to explain a telegram he had just received. It followed by one day the almost fatal accident that had felled Fritz Kreisler during his crossing of one of New York's streets. The telegram read, "Today a great artist was critically injured. Too bad it could not have been you." The signature at the end of the message was that of the bass player who had been sent from the stage! We put our heads together, thrown into consternation by the explanation we would have to make. Just then, Richard Burgin was glimpsed near the doorway to Koussevitzky's room. I immediately called to him; we thrust the telegram into his hands and asked him to explain in Russian its contents. We never knew what he told Koussevitzky.

The message was purported to have been sent at 6:45 a.m. from an address on Commonwealth Avenue. We asked the Boston Police Department for assistance. Nothing was ever forthcoming. The particular apartment house at the address given had a telephone in its lobby, locked to all until 9:00 a.m.! It appeared obvious to us that no player was going to send such a message and be foolish enough to sign his own name. We were never to discover the real sender. But in a few days, Koussevitzky had evidently determined that someone was trying to make further trouble for the player. Rogers was summoned to the balcony overlooking the stage and instructed to send a message to the missing bassist and ask him to return. Peace was restored, and perhaps Koussevitzky felt a glow of warmth from his own magnanimous gesture.

In 1945, there was no Berkshire Festival due to restrictions placed by the government on any outdoor gatherings of people. The pupils at Tanglewood could give their smaller concerts more or less privately, but the Festival as such was cancelled for the summer. But about the same time, our Tanglewood Quartet received a telegram that invited us to appear in Lenox to take part in a very special celebration that was to observe the 175th anniversary of the Church on the Hill. We were to be free of our Pops responsibilities for several days while we honored this request.

Later on, we went to Lenox and met with Koussevitzky in his house on the hill. As first citizen of Lenox, Koussevitzky had been invited to make the main speech of the afternoon's program. He expressed his hope that we would play a Haydn quartet, and then after the speech had reached its conclusion, we should perform Tchaikovsky's *Andante cantabile*, to bring the program to its proper end.

He was very explicit about our moment. We would play the first quartet, then "I vill make it my speech. Ven I say, "_____," you vill immediately blay *Andante cantabile*." We marked the last sentence of his speech on our music so that we might not miss our cue.

The celebration reached its peak on Sunday afternoon, and it was what might be called a "scorcher." We sat, surrounded by the flowers suitable to the occasion, on a small platform normally used by the minister. Our Haydn quartet went well, op. 77, no.1, I recall. Then Koussevitzky rose to make his speech. We sat with our eyes glued to the sentence that would be our cue. It never came. Koussevitzky quit speaking; then in the silence that ensued, we heard his "Nu?" A faster beginning for this piece was probably never before known. We were never to learn what his last sentence had actually been or why he had suddenly changed his thought.

The next morning, we felt it best to call on him, to let him know we appreciated his asking us up for the occasion. We found him at ease in the house on the hill. He indicated chairs for us, and we fell into general conversation. The question was asked by Rolland Tapley as to what he was finding to occupy his time now that there was no festival. "I haf found new vorks to play, even by Mozart. I haf discovered a Mozart symphony, also in G minor, just as good as the famous one."

With this, our cellist Karl Zeise remarked that when he was in Philadelphia, Leopold Stokowski was constantly discovering and bringing out hitherto unplayed works. "Ah yes, Stokowski, a great talent. In 1924, he was the number one conductor of America. Don I came and now dere vere two great conductors in America."

During a rehearsal of an organ concerto when E. Power Biggs was officiating at the organ, the organ console had been placed in its usual position at a spot somewhat removed from the conductor's position. Koussevitzky suddenly requested, "Biggs, come closer. I cannot hear you." The console was moved closer to him, and he seemed to be satisfied although the amount of sound from Biggs was not one whit more!

We were rehearsing the Sowerby Organ Concerto with Biggs, already at the end of our rehearsal time, as we came to the end of the slow movement of the work. As the final chords were given, Koussevitzky asked for the organ to play alone. Perfect! Now the orchestra was asked to play alone. Perfect! Now the entire ensemble! "I hear a G, please organ alone." Perfect. Now orchestra. Perfect. Now everyone. "I hear a G." The chord we were playing was one in D flat that does not contain a G. We kept at it, several times with the same result, until Jacobus Langendoen, a cellist, said in some exasperation, "Cut it out. We've had enough." His stand partner was playing a very high harmonic in place of the note he should have been playing. Just an instance of certain players trying to plague the conductor. Koussevitzky reasoned that it must be a "ceepher" (cipher) on the instrument. Of course, it was never heard again.

I have read quite recently that there seems to be a feud between conductors and instrumentalists. Perhaps there is a modicum of truth hidden somewhere in that statement. But players do not openly or intentionally declare themselves in defiance of the conductor standing before them. They take his measure in a few moments. Of course, we must not forget that an orchestra of some 110 players holds just that many opinions of how the standard work should be played. They have formed opinions based on the many fine performances they have known, through the conducting of the best men before the public. A young man of thirty-five now proposes (in some instances) to show them how much better his performance will be than what they have been used to. Unconsciously, an orchestra plays with less than usual conviction, unwilling to let itself accede to the requests of this young upstart.

I have observed that anyone attempting to lead a large symphony orchestra is well endowed with that quality we may well call conceit, some to an extent beyond their ability to justify. It is all well and good for a conductor to have confidence in what he can do, especially if he can do it when needed, but beyond that, he is simply shown up as one who should not have been there in the first place.

During my span in the Boston Symphony, we saw conductors who were wonderful in their niche and others who could not be called conductors by any stretch of the imagination. I believe the low point was reached when a quite well-known personality who fancied himself a conductor asked us, "You start, fellows, and I'll catch you." This same gentleman managed to conduct his way through a Russian dance, all the way giving the beat in exactly the reverse order. Of course, we corrected the playing on the spot, and no one in the audience was the wiser.

These gentlemen seem to be a necessary part of an orchestra's existence. They come in all ages, standing before us, ready to expose their bag of tricks. In some cases with greatness; in others, hardly mediocre. An orchestra of seasoned players can take a guest conductor's measure in very short order, hardly more than five minutes for a quick estimate, little more for a more permanent judgment. They see how he first faces them, what he says, how he grasps his baton, the tempo at which he begins one of the great works, how he controls the balance of sections. There are so many small things that reveal the conductor as he really is. He is better accepted, usually, if we know that his instrument has been one of those commonly used in such an organization as he has elected to lead.

A pianist, no matter how capable on his chosen instrument, does not show up well as a conductor of an orchestra unless he has had to face those moments when called upon to play one of those other instruments himself and to know the inherent difficulty, especially when his guest conducting may not be of the highest caliber.

On the opposite end of the roster, there are those who completely justified their position before us. Fine musicians in whatever instrument they have chosen, full of the experiences of many years, they are usually well aware of the players' individual instrumental problems and wish to bring all the disparate difficulties into a sensible whole that will produce a performance of the highest musical caliber. To such as they, an orchestra will respond with playing, although different from what they are used to, that will fall within that level that we all recognize as high art. This is the end desired by all.

It is interesting to observe what usually happens during the rehearsal periods before an actual performance. A guest conductor, especially the younger one, arrives full of ideas of how a masterwork should sound. Often his conception is based on one he has heard through the phonograph—an easy way to learn a composition today. Occasionally, it is based on performances of another great orchestra in whose vicinity he has happened to dwell. He is sure that he knows the work thoroughly, perhaps even to the point where he may be able to show the august group before which he now stands a thing or two about tempi, balances, etc.—all the many variables inherent in the great works of the masters.

So he begins. Perhaps he notes a difference in the response of this orchestra to his commands. But it can't all be done in one rehearsal! Tomorrow, he will bring them a little nearer to his wishes. However, he is aware that these men do indeed already know their jobs. The next rehearsal sees him insisting less on what he thought he wanted; however, all is going smoothly. By the time the last rehearsal is over or his first concert with them is being played, the orchestra knows full well that they are actually playing the work as they knew it. The young conductor feels, perhaps smugly, that he has brought about this miracle of sound. But the reins have simply been taken out of his hands very quietly. Through the fine playing of a great orchestra many a reputation has been made for a young conductor.

Players recognize that through the manipulation of a mute piece of stick, conductors gain a reputation for sounds they have no way of making. Every sound heard comes from one or another of the players, never from that wand the conductor holds. He can make no mistake. That has to be done by the player(s). The guilty player must take the blame while the conductor receives (and accepts) the plaudits of the audience. Poor man to have to accept poor playing from one of the musicians before him. Few listeners realize that often these mistakes on the musician's part may be due to faulty direction on the part of the leader or from a situation that has created nervousness at the moment of playing.

Players recognize this injustice. They see that generally a conductor does little more than give cues to one player or another, thinking that sufficient for the performance by the orchestra. Even these pointings of the baton produce no sound from the conductor. We have all seen that a trained seal can choose the correct bell or button to push that will result in a tone. At least he does produce a sound!

But there were giants among conductors. We were to see quite a few of them.

Sir Adrian Boult made a guest appearance with us not too long after I had joined the orchestra. His conducting was masterly, of course, but he added more than a bit of himself and his English rearing. The personal ingredient was readily recognizable by the players, and their responses to such as Boult's could not fail to result in an especially splendid concert.

Koussevitzky sat, as usual, in his seat near the second door of the first balcony right. We were always aware of this presence there when we had guest conductors with us. After Boult's departure, Koussevitzky returned to us on the following Monday morning. He greeted us by congratulating us on our performance of the preceding week. "I congrotulate you for your playing of a splendid concert. I listened you from my seat. But the brass vas not in tune. The sonorité of my orchestra vas not there. The percussion vas not in tune; the bassi vere out of tune. It vas so bad I had to go home!" At a later concert several years later, when Boult again conducted, he delivered this statement, "You like Mozart dot vay? I hate it." We thought it had been especially fine.

During a visit by Fritz Reiner, we came to our Saturday evening performance. We were, at that time, broadcasting for Allis-Chalmers, as I remember. The work at hand was Richard Strauss's *Symphonia domestica*. All seemed to be going well, Reiner in complete command, when Rolland Tapley rose from his position in the first violin section.

With his violin in one hand and a piece of music in the other, he made his way toward our side of the stage. Directly in front of Reiner he passed. The conductor paid him no heed. Tapley continued until he had reached the position of the timpanist, Szulc, then settled on the right side of the stage. He handed the music to Szulc then turned and made his way back to his own chair on the other side of the stage.

At no time did Reiner pay him the slightest attention. Tapley had come upon the timpani part where it had been mistakenly placed by the librarian. Watching Szulc's face, he had seen his start of panic when no timpani part was there to play from. There was nothing else for Tapley to do.

In the season of 1946-1947, Bruno Walter came to us. Why we had not seen him before, we could not really know. Perhaps there was more than a little truth to the suspicion that his reputation was too great. Koussevitzky simply hadn't felt he wished his presence. I can't say that this was true, however. But when he did appear, there was not a moment of indecision on anyone's part. Here was a conductor.

With him, we worked beautifully, and several concerts of the highest order were given. I remember that he labeled the Mozart G minor symphony as the "sad symphony" of Mozart. I thought at the time that I wished I had twenty or more years to play under this conductor, but better judgment showed me that this could not be, for Walter, already over seventy years of age, had suffered heart attacks that forced him to apportion his work to stay within the limit of what he could do. But he was supreme.

Musicians can be forgiven if they often ask the question, of what use is the conductor? What actually is his function? Why should he reap an income far in excess of what we consider him worth? And in some respects, each of these questions has a legitimate reason for being asked. It is entirely possible for an orchestra to play many of the masterworks of the literature without a conductor. It has been tried and proven. I much prefer, however, someone up front who will do his task of keeping us together by occasionally indicating tempo, a dynamic or two along the way, etc. I think a conductor is sort of necessary, but not to the extent he is considered to be so by the audiences. Of course, there are those whose presence makes a greater success of a performance than it might have been without them. To such men, an orchestra will respond with all it has to give. But the list of such men is not a long one.

In America, the star system has made the person who is named musical director of an orchestra a very important figure, regardless of his true worth. If he can be observed to be one who makes a stunning appearance on the podium, he has already gone a considerable distance in forming his own public, those who will rush to his rescue should detracting voices be heard. Perhaps this very ability to be well looked upon sartorially may be counted a considerable asset to the orchestra management that has hired him, but it actually is of no use to the orchestra players in their performance of whatever they may be called upon to play. The reward to them is simply that his popularity may result in more ticket sales, which of course means more income and better guaranteed salaries than otherwise.

The conductor's function is to see that the orchestra sections coordinate themselves as directed by the score in front of him. He can give indications, commonly called cues, inject a bit more of himself and his idea of what the composer may have meant (as he sees it), on occasion causing a performance to be better than it might have been without a conductor. The planning of the season's programs is also his responsibility, as well as the study of those scores to be played. Of course, it is a lot of work, but so is the playing of any instrument of the orchestra that he leads. But this in itself is no excuse for the extraordinary amounts paid by one management or another to those in charge of their local orchestras.

I recall the first appearance of Dmitri Mitropoulos. His memory was startling, and his conducting from memory was the first example of this sort of thing we had witnessed. He went on to the Minneapolis Symphony and was very successful in his career.

George Szell was another conductor of high attainments. He had actually been a pianist before turning to conducting but had managed to equip himself to handle a symphony orchestra in a very workmanlike and artistic manner. He was looked upon as something of a martinet, reflecting on his Prussian militaristic rearing. He remained with the Cleveland Orchestra, bringing it to a high state of perfection.

It was during the war years, and we were arriving in Chicago. At the time, it was no easy matter to secure a taxicab from the station, for they were very scarce; and the demand was very great. One boarded from either door, since it seemed to be first come, first serve. During this particular tour, John Burk, our famous program annotator, had been asked to accompany the orchestra and see to the comforts of our leader. Burk was a very gentle soul, not given to pushing himself in if he felt he was intruding. So he took his turn in line and eventually secured a cab for Koussevitzky and himself. He opened the door and stood aside for Koussevitzky to seat himself. But from the other door, another taxi seeker had entered. His first words were, "Move over, Pop," these to Koussevitzky, who was not in the habit of hearing himself addressed thusly. John Burk knew this and, without attempting any words of argument with the newcomer, simply took Koussevitzky by the arm and removed him from his seat. They took a later taxi.

Koussevitzky's annual winter vacation usually consisted of a short stay in a warmer climate, and on one occasion, he had chosen to rest on an island somewhere off the coast of Virginia. He came back in fine fettle and in a very jovial mood. The work he had chosen to play upon his return was Debussy's *La mer*. At rehearsal, we had reached the last movement, I remember. There was a moment when the third trumpet has to give out a call, an interval of a major second. As it did so, Koussevitzky stopped us to remark, "I haf, all my life, vondered vat Debussy mean in this place. Last week, I sat by my vindow on my island. I heard a bird over the vater make such a melody. I turned to my little black girl—." He got no further, the orchestra breaking into smiles and laughter. He did not know how to accept this response. Looking rather nettled, he said, "I vill never tell you another story." So there were moments when smiles and laughter could be heard, but they were so unusual that it is far more true to say that jokes or humor had no place in our life in Symphony Hall, at least where Koussevitzky was concerned. His attention was completely given to his personal career and that of "my orchestra."

In Koussevitzky's day, recordings were made on wax discs. We had to play 4 1/2 minutes without error, otherwise the disc was spoiled; and we would have to play the selection over—sometimes more than once until a perfect disc should be realized. Not yet had the modern recording tapes been invented, which would allow us to play a small portion of the music until a perfect remake had been produced, one that would be spliced into the whole for a perfect performance.

Playing in this manner was sure to be a nerve-wracking ordeal. Koussevitzky's attention was fixed on reproducing for the records the exact sound he was used to getting during a performance. He felt that the orchestra must play as usual, and the recording equipment should be used to permanently "print" the music as he had heard it himself.

During those early years of our work with RCA, Charles O'Connell was the man in charge of RCA's machinery that was housed in one of the upstairs rooms. Communication was largely by loud speaker. Only occasionally would O'Connell show himself on the stage. Koussevitzky might communicate with him by speaking into a microphone with such a question as "Mr. O'Connell, how many long the time was?"

After O'Connell's departure from RCA, his replacement was Macklin Marrow, a chap who was somewhat of a conductor himself, which O'Connell was definitely not. Early in his career with us, Marrow felt that a recording was not to his liking, and he descended to the stage and suggested to Koussevitzky that such and such a moment could use more of some section of the wind groups since the recording was not coming through as he would wish. Placing a hand on Marrow's shoulder, Koussevitzky answered, "My dear, you go back to your apparat. I vill take care down here." Marrow never again approached Koussevitzky with such a request. As a matter of fact, he was soon replaced in that position. I have no doubt that the "apparat" was manipulated by the engineers upstairs to help them secure what they felt was the needed balance.

During a Berkshire Festival season, we were informed that we were to make a film that would be used by our state department to extol the beauties of both Tanglewood and America. Our part in it would be to perform some work of sufficient length to show the orchestra in all its splendor. The work chosen to be used was Beethoven's "Egmont Overture."

Exigencies of the technical practices of that day demanded that we first record the work, playing as usual. After a good recording had been made, we would only then make the film to be used in connection with the music already in the can. We were to take our accustomed places in the orchestra, dressed as for a concert, and while Koussevitzky conducted, we were to make the motions we normally used but were to make no sound in doing so. So simple, it seemed.

The music was turned on, and the cameras began to grind. One would have supposed that Koussevitzky, who had only the day before so skillfully recorded what we now heard, would have no difficulty in simulating the conducting motions he had used. Not so! He was a man of moods, and his mood of this day was different from that of yesterday! He conducted in a different tempo, so his movements were certainly out of synchronization with the music we were hearing. In only a moment or two, disaster had struck. We were forced to try it again. Mystified, Koussevitzky asked of the technicians why the "apparat" did not follow him. Eventually, by doing small snatches of the overture, we got through the work, and the final film produced abounded in cuts that would allow our playing to approximate to an extent that which appeared to be taking place on the stage. Koussevitzky was always certain that it was the fault of the "apparat."

Koussevitzky had a genius for selecting material that caused his programs to continue to appeal not only to the players but to the audiences. He seemed to have a genius for choosing the selections that go so well together. A listener might find a work, one of the newer works, which he could find little cause to enjoy, but the main work on the same program would wipe away unhappiness engendered by its performance and send this same listener from the hall with a spirit of elation that he had been fortunate enough to have heard music to elevate his soul.

The alphabet of music is inadequate to truly show what the composer might have in mind. The conductor, however, without personal collaboration with the composer, must take from the score the thoughts he feels the composer must have meant. These are flavored by his own background of nationality, his musical training (as an orchestral player, hopefully), his experience in conducting elsewhere, and the innate ability to reach his players in thought or ideas, to convince them that their performances must glow with inspiration at all times. But there must still remain a certain humility, which all great men show, that there is a pinnacle the conductor strives for. Having such a conductor at their helm, the players respond with performances that are often out of this world.

Koussevitzky, although he believed that he himself knew the only way to conduct many of the masterworks, also possessed with his attendant conceit a certain humility toward the art that he served. I shall speak of it a bit later.

One of our players, a percussionist in charge of small sounds such as those of the glockenspiel, triangle, and various of the small chimes, had become so uncertain of what Koussevitzky wished that he found himself unable to approach any of these instruments for fear that he would be criticized. He was not wrong in this supposition. I have watched him as he prepared to play a very small note in the *Afternoon of a Faun*. He would grasp his right hand with his left in preparation, then at the proper moment would release his right and make the stroke, immediately regrasping his right hand with his left to control the shaking. At one moment, Koussevitzky spoke to him, "My dear, I haf been vondering all dese years vot to call you, and now I haf a name for you. You are a 'killer,' a killer of all the vonderful sounds that ve made. I vill be glad to see you go." And this chap was a very fine player. Something had happened along the way to bring about such feeling from the conductor.

I have estimated that in my playing life with the Boston Symphony, I have taken part in about thirty definitive performances of each of the great works of the literature, these in addition to the performances that I had come to feel were the ultimate expressions of these same great works.

As time passes in one's career, one begins to wonder just what the composer may have had in mind when composing the work. From innumerable performances with the same orchestra under its permanent conductor, one becomes bewildered as these definitive performances pile one upon another. Almost a hostility can be generated during a performance one is forced to suffer through at the hands of a guest conductor of less than the highest caliber. The conductor may pass lightly over the very moments that have made the work so great, exhibit an apathetic feeling during the playing of certain phrases, each in themselves of great beauty. His tempi may make it impossible to properly negotiate passagework that is of prime importance for the best presentation of the work. He often glosses over it.

Of course, in the final analysis, all the sounds are made by the players. A conductor standing alone on a stage would look ridiculous, indeed, if he stood there conducting without an orchestra. His baton would be useless as a musical instrument! It is, of course, necessary to have a proper collaboration between conductor and orchestra before the great beauties of whatever composition are to be heard. And it galls the players when the eventual applause seems meant for the conductor alone. But only he can win, for if a player blows or bows a false note, it is rather certain who will have to take the blame. Not the conductor!

Tempi are really relative. What is an allegro, a largo? And just what is meant by mezzo forte? This last nuance is probably responsible for more indecision than any other marking I can name. Koussevitzky put it that "mezzo forte is the most baddest nuance qui existe," with which I feel that most players or conductors are apt to agree.

During the era of which I am writing, there were indeed players in the Boston Symphony who actually knew or worked with such as Ravel and Debussy while they were composing their finest masterpieces. Debussy died only in 1918. Ravel lived until 1937 or a little later. I can remember Ravel sitting in our first balcony listening to our rehearsal of one of his compositions. If memory serves me, it was *Le tombeau de Couperin*.

With such men in his orchestra, Koussevitzky had an easier time than another conductor might have had, whose only acquaintance with the music to be played was through the score before him. Such players as Gillet, Laurent, Allard, Valkenier, and Speyer, plus a number of string players who had served their apprenticeship in Paris, could bring to their performances exactly the flavor the composer wanted. The additional inspiration injected into their playing by the admonitions offered by Koussevitzky could not fail to create extraordinary performances of these newer works. But Koussevitzky did not stop there. He continued to exhort them to their greatest efforts in the playing of the masterworks of the literature, to a result certainly not equaled by any other orchestra of which we had knowledge.

One of our Carnegie Hall concerts was so immediately successful that the conductor was recalled several times more than usual. As he came out for what he knew would be the final recall, he said in an aside to Richard Burgin as he bowed, "Sometimes, I even amaze myself."

In the early years of Tanglewood, Koussevitzky used to visit the tents that some of the orchestra members had erected down at the lake at the foot of the Tanglewood property. Customarily used by the Lenox Brotherhood, the camping area was vacated by them during the Festival and made available for our use. Those who liked to camp had thought it a splendid opportunity to enjoy the outdoors, save a bit of their per diem (expense money), and had erected their private tents. In some cases, those who enjoyed cooking their special dishes found opportunity. Generally, these players were of European backgrounds and more specifically of French origin. There is no question that they were very capable chefs. In some special cases, they felt their cooking was good enough to warrant inviting Koussevitzky to be their guest. He often accepted their invitations.

On this plot of ground stood a huge birch tree, said to be the largest in all of Massachusetts. At the foot of this tree was a circular formation of stones, obviously a planned formation. We had been told that the circular formation marked the meeting place of innumerable meetings of Indians many years past, and was called the council fire.

Leslie Rogers, our librarian, was an inveterate collector of Americana. He had concluded that he had come upon a wonderful spot in which to find arrowheads or other artifacts. This should be a veritable goldmine. Unfortunately, he did not hesitate to make known his intention. When the moment came for him to begin his digging, he found himself surrounded by his orchestral "friends," not there to help dig, but to watch Rogers at this work.

As shovelful succeeded shovelful and nothing came to light, Rogers found that not only his energy was dissipated, but also his ambition. Still, there was face to be saved, and he couldn't quit until he had discovered at least a little of something. He decided to go down one more foot than the several he had already reached. Driving his shovel into the ground again, he was rewarded with the feel of some solid object to be unearthed. "Ah, now I can show them I knew what I was talking about." "Them" was the group of his colleagues who had now become hecklers of a sort. Swiftly, the object came to light, and to Roger's amazement and disappointment, it turned out to be an empty whiskey bottle, and one not old enough to have been placed there by any Indian who might have visited the spot. The laughter that greeted his find had more than a little to do with Roger's losing his ambition. I never heard of his conducting another "dig."

With the end of the war, those players who had been drafted were once again in their old positions. Came the moment when Koussevitzky singled out one of these returnees, and fixing him with his eye, he said, "My dear, you vere a captain in the army?" No answer expected.

"And ven the general gif you a order, you had to follow it? Vell, it is the same in a orchestra. Ven the general gif the captain a order, he must obey it. I am the general, and you are the captain. Ven I ask you for something, you must gif me vot I ask. Dot is the true democratical vay!" At the end of that season, the captain left the orchestra.

We were often admonished to:

"You must boil. I must haf a ocean of sound."

"Ee don't go. Please, to the last atom."

In a moment of exasperation, he remarked:

"If you do not blay bedder, I vill resign!" A later moment might cause him to cry, "No, I vill not resign. *You* vill resign!"

In a moment of exaltation while playing the "Great Gate of Kiev" from Moussorgsky's, *Pictures at an Exhibition*, it was often in rehearsal that he would call out, "I haf heard the bells."

He was very conscious of the sanctity of his calling. He could not stand inattention of any kind from any player. On one occasion, he noticed a player moving his jaws. At him he shouted, "This is not a cafeteria." Then, pointing to the ceiling, "This is our cathedral."

To another player who seemed to be taking a little too long to seat himself and get ready to play: "Made yourself comfortable, or do you need a nurse?"

Bothered by the performance of the triangle player, he asked, "Who blay the triangolo?" Then espying the offender, "Ah, a guest triller."

In the very later years of his reign, Koussevitzky decided that he would make a change in the viola section. Jean Lefranc was demoted from his position as first viola and replaced by Jean Cauhape, in spite of the fact that Lefranc had announced his decision to retire. Nevertheless, in that, his final year, he was compelled to sit beside his successor in what appeared to us as truly a gesture of spite on Koussevitzky's part. Only after several weeks of the season, Cauhape was summoned into Koussevitzky's room.

"Cauhape, you think you blay vell?"

Silence.

"Not at all."

Silence.

"You blay like a man with a little sight leading the blind."

Not a compliment to the rest of us, of course.

As Koussevitzky's conductorship began to reach its twenty-fifth year, he evidently felt that he should relinquish his baton to a younger man. We had now been in the union for five years or so. He had already come to the conclusion that it was not what he had expected. He complained that "I am around with ice." The reduction of all our gentlemen's agreements with the trustees to the written word had now given the players the power to go against his wishes if they so inclined, and this new strength was evidenced in the faces of many of the players about him. We had taken from him the freedom to have his Thursday morning audiences, for one. "You are drunk with power," he shouted on one occasion. So came the moment when he met with the trustees. He informed them that he would like to conduct only a half-season and pass over his baton to Leonard Bernstein, then a coming conductor on the orchestral scene.

To this, he received the answer that the trustees could not do as he wished since Mr. Bernstein was a comparative unknown, though talented, and had little repertoire or reputation. With that, Koussevitzky suggested that the other half of the season be given to two young men, Bernstein and Eleazor Cavalho, another young conductor from South America. Both of these young men had been his students at Tanglewood.

Prominent in this discussion was the newer trustee, Judge Jacob Kaplan. Judge Kaplan was acting as spokesman for the trustees at that moment. When informed that his wishes could not be complied with, Judge Kaplan further informed him that, "Doctor Koussevitzky, we do not wish you to conduct less, we wish you to conduct more." Koussevitzky answered that if he could not have his wish granted, "I vill resign." That brought the answer from Kaplan, "Your resignation is accepted." And so it was.

During that last year of Koussevitzky's reign, programs continued to be as interesting as always, with certain newer works interspersed with the classics, but there came a moment when our program was to feature Tchaikovsky's Sixth Symphony, the *Pathétique*. One might have supposed that in this last year with us, he would have given it little more than passing attention. Certainly, his name was linked with this composition more closely than with any other. He was noted for his treatment of it, his ability to wring from it the last of its moods, setting apart his performance from those of any other conductor.

As we began the first rehearsal for the coming performance, he took the score in hand, opened it, and announced, "Ve must see vot it is." He had not yet become satisfied that he had fully understood all that Tchaikovsky had written. A remark such as that could not fail to move the players who had followed him through the many, many attempts to wrest from the score all the beauties and meanings intended by the composer. I could not help but admire the dedication this remark implied. On April 29, his last program included Beethoven's first and last symphonies. He announced to us that "With me, go the last true tradition of the Beethoven retard."

Koussevitzky was to visit us as guest conductor during the remainder of his life. His major interest, aside from Tanglewood, was in attempting to build the Israel Philharmonic Orchestra, and he spent considerable time with that orchestra in the ensuing months. When he first returned as a guest, he felt, during rehearsal, that he should speak to a solo player who had joined the orchestra since his retirement. To his surprise, the newer player answered with a remark of his own. Koussevitzky, with some sorrow in his voice, a bit of asperity as well, told us that "now I feel like a guest conductor."

All who knew Tanglewood or had occasion to visit it during those years of Koussevitzky's complete control of all things the Boston Symphony was trying to do, had become familiar with his majestic figure. He made an outstanding picture. He usually wore a suit of light color, shoes immaculately shined, his Russian cape draped over his shoulders. This attire was set off by a jaunty cap of white. He would look in on any rehearsal in progress, make a remark or two perhaps, and continue on to the next point that might excite his interest. One never knew just where or when to expect him.

Koussevitzky's last illness overtook him while he was vacationing in Arizona. According to the story we heard from one who claimed to have been witness to it, Koussevitzky felt sick enough to warrant calling a doctor. The doctor frankly told him that he was suffering from leukemia, or cancer of the blood. Upon hearing this, Koussevitzky asked, "How many long de time I haf?"

"About three months," came the doctor's reply.

"I vill not accept!" shouted Koussevitzky. But within days, he took to his bed. Exactly three months to the day, June 4, 1951, he fell from his bed and died of what was diagnosed as a cerebral hemorrhage. He would have been seventy-seven years of age on July 26.

Koussevitzky's passing was marked by suitable ceremonies. In Boston, his funeral services were of a combined nature, Greek Orthodox and Episcopalian, held at the Church of the Advent. His body was removed to Lenox, where, after appropriate ceremonies, it was interred in the cemetery of the Church on the Hill, Congregational. There a very special location is given to his resting place. Under a very large tree, he rests beside the grave of his wife, Natalia, now also by that of his last wife, Olga. There are no indications on the stone that marks the grave that he ever had anything to do with the Boston Symphony Orchestra, for the large stone was given by the Israel Philharmonic Orchestra in grateful memory of his assistance in helping create their own organization. It makes one ponder. Yearly ceremonies at the graveside are held by those associated with the Berkshire Music Center. July 26 is duly observed.

Most of the photographs shown here of my father and the orchestra are from the Boston Symphony archives. They were made available to me through the kindness of Bridget Carr, the archivist of the Symphony, and Barbara Perkel, her assistant.

By permission of the Boston Symphony

Soon after my father joined the orchestra, the Symphony in 1936 published a book of charcoal drawings, along with short biographical sketches, of each member of the orchestra. The drawings were done by Gerome Brush, a contemporary artist. This portrait is the one he did of my father for the collection.

The biographical sketch (most of which is inaccurate) reads,

> "All aboard for Natchez, Cairo, and St. Louis!" Yes, his family were railroad people; for a time he was a brakeman himself. He didn't mind the cinders; it was the monotony. If you are a musician and a railroad man, the rhythm in the click of the rails can seem pretty ironical.
>   Mr. George Norwood Humphrey is from Ohio. He was born in 1904. He graduated from the New England Conservatory with honors. Railroad time instead of 4/4 time a while after that. Nevertheless, the day came when Mr. Humphrey rode as a passenger to join the Minneapolis Orchestra, and since 1934 he has been in the Boston Symphony.

My father, mother, and I in Somerville, Massachusetts, October 1934.

The Tanglewood Quartet in the late 1950s. Standing from left to right: Karl Zeise, cello; Stanley Benson, second violin; Rolland Tapley, first violin; and George Humphrey, viola. Jesus Maria Sanroma is the pianist. Malcolm Holmes, the original second violinist, had died in 1953.

Boston Symphony string players meeting at one of their homes to play quartets. From left to right: Robert Gundersen, first violin; Manuel Zung, second violin; Jacobus Langendoen, cello; and George Humphrey, viola.

My father, a skilled luthier, working on one of his instruments.

My father and Karl Zeise reviewing a score.

My father and Karl Zeise in discussion with Charles Munch about the formation of the Icelandic-American Quartet with two Icelanders for a goodwill tour.

Serge Koussevitzky.

Koussevitzky at the podium.

Koussevitzky with the first chair players in the early years of his conductorship. Front, left to right: Fernand (Jean) Gillet, oboe; Richard Burgin, concertmaster; George Mager, trumpet; Serge Koussevitzky; Georges Laurent, flute; and Jean Bedetti, cello. Rear, left to right: Jean Lefranc, viola; Victor Polatschek, clarinet; Raymond Allard, bassoon; Wilhelm Valkenier, French horn; and Jacob Raichman, trombone.

Pierre Monteux, Serge Koussevitzky, and Charles Munch in January 1951 on the first appearance of Monteux as guest conductor.

Richard Burgin, concertmaster.

Charles Van Wynbergen, viola (1910-1951).

My father and Charles Van Wynbergen at Tanglewood in October 1936.

Danny Kaye, addressing a Symphony Hall audience. © Heinz H. Weissenstein/Whitestone Photo—All Rights Reserved

Boston Symphony members in Red Square, Moscow, in front of the cracked bell, September 1956. From left to right, Sheldon Rotenberg, Manuel Zung, Einar Hansen (rear), Arthur Press, George Humphrey (camera), Harold Farberman (rear), Alfred Krips, Louis Speyer (rear), and Alfred Zighera. The rightmost man is unidentified.

My father dressed as an eighteenth-century musician for a Pension Fund concert on February 1, 1939, when the orchestra performed Haydn's "Farewell Symphony."

My father and mother in Japan with some Japanese friends in 1969.

CHAPTER 3

The Munch Years

With the beginning of the 1949-1950 season, Charles Munch took over the helm. From his first words to us, we learned that, "We must have joy with our music or I go." This was greeted with the greatest pleasure by the orchestra. It seemed about time that we should enjoy our work, instead of living in fear while we were doing it. We had lived through those many years of tyranny, despotism, and dictatorship, surviving to the point where we might look forward to other years when our music making would be of some pleasure. So we faced with great anticipation the coming of this man by whom we were enthralled.

He was completely unlike Koussevitzky in appearance. A very large person whose height must have been somewhat over six feet, a body in proportion, capped by a face of almost benign appearance, yet very intelligent overall.

He used both German and French in speaking to the orchestra, his knowledge of English being but a smattering. He was to try desperately to master it sufficiently to communicate with us, but in his frustration at one moment he declared English to be a "language of the pigs."

Munch was unquestionably a well-schooled and experienced conductor, with certain predilections that gave his conducting gestures a nature inseparable from the man himself. He was heard to say to us that if he could, he would ask for large splotches of sound from the orchestra, as though he were throwing paint at a canvas, a la Delacroix. His gestures indicated his desires.

His background had been of combined French and German forebears. Hailing from Strasbourg in Alsace Lorraine, he was completely Alsatian. His repertoire was to reveal that he was equally at home with the German and the French composers, each of which he was able to conduct superlatively. He had been a violinist himself, having served as concertmaster of the Strasbourg Orchestra and had many times been soloist with that and other orchestras of Europe.

His first program included *La procession nocturne* of Henri Rabaud, a former conductor of the Boston Symphony Orchestra, a Handel organ concerto with E. Power Biggs as soloist, and Beethoven's Fifth Symphony. This was a program that showed at once his ability to deal with the great delicacy of French writing, as well as the huge power of the Beethoven work.

Looking back over the programs of Munch's era, it is evident that in that first year we were given a preview of what was to come. He performed works by Rabaud, Handel, Beethoven, Rachmaninoff, Messaien, Copland, Mozart, Berlioz, Pfitzner, Wagner, Haydn, Honegger, Milhaud, Mendelsohn, d'Indy, Foss, Strauss, Saint-Saëns, Bach, Harris, V. Thompson, and Brahms.

Quite soon after he became our conductor, we began to notice that he did not like to rehearse. Sometimes, after a few moments of rehearsal, he would shout, "Pas necessaire!" and dismiss us for the day or suddenly cancel a rehearsal scheduled for later that same day. He also hated repeats in the music. He would tell us, "The world knows this music. Why must we play it twice? Please, no repeat." This would be an order to omit the repeat from the performance as well.

The orchestra, rebounding from the years of Koussevitzky, loved this sort of treatment, for many older players had already had enough of some of the masterworks they had played so many, many times. But, of course, this is not the proper way to keep an orchestra at its peak and signs soon began to appear that the standard was falling. Even within that first year, there were unmistakable signs that we had lost something that had always been taken for granted by the older players. We never knew exactly what to expect. Rehearsals were too short to allow us to learn what Munch wished. He was definitely a man of the moment. He could give an inspiring performance of any of the music with which he felt a sympathy; then the next day that same music would take on a lackluster quality that could not fail to be boring. Yet the orchestra retained a great part of what it had been with Koussevitzky and could play a magnificent performance if it was not interfered with.

With the last note of a concert, Munch would run from the stage and disappear down the stairway to the street. He drove his Oldsmobile 88 at a very fast clip from Symphony Hall to his Milton home. If he did not drive, his valet, Roger, took over the wheel, and they shot away from the hall as though the devil was after them. No more holding court for the plaudits of the old ladies in his audience.

We very soon learned that he was, indeed, a very large musician in other senses than that of his size. He had a comprehension, a sympathy for, and the ability to handle the most difficult scores. The baton technique Koussevitzky lacked was his without seeming difficulty. No longer did we have to try to make up the extra time in measures of uneven meters. Munch actually indicated them in an unmistakable manner, and we could simply play what we had before us. And he was able to conduct a score from memory when occasion demanded it. He would often avail himself of the privilege, especially in the works of Stravinsky or Honegger, music with which he was completely conversant and felt a sympathy for. This is not to say he was infallible. Of course, he made errors, but the orchestra could cover up in such a way that the audience was never aware of the temporary lapse in his memory.

This very freedom from a score gave a musical sweep to what he did and caused the great differences between one performance and another. We began to gain a great flexibility. We had to be prepared to do anything that he might demand for this concert, but not wish for the next. This sort of thing can make one almost as nervous as the other well-prepared version under an autocrat.

How difficult to draw a parallel between the two men, one a hardworking taskmaster, the other an impulsive creature of the moment. To a man, the players fell in love with our new conductor, though we could not fail to recognize his inadequacies. We saw that he was a very untidy individual, not in his personal habits, but in his manner of rehearsing. He seemed to be more interested in the whole picture than in any details of that same picture.

Now we were not asked to produce sounds that went further to describe the music than could be called for in the score. We were not asked for pianissimo so soft that one could hardly hear or play them. And we were subjected to tempi so fast that would make it almost impossible to negotiate passagework of an important nature.

But we loved him. So tender was he, so efficient! We saw that we had with us a terrific musician, one who was completely up to his task, and who simply reveled in producing beautiful music without the agony and pain of the necessary rehearsals. But this cannot be! It is truly necessary to undergo the hours of rehearsal if one expects to really perform this great music as honestly as possible. Anything less is eventually very unsatisfactory.

Munch, as I have said, was a huge man. His feet, in particular, seemed outlandishly large. His entrance to and exit from the stage were almost of a running nature. We always expected him to fall in his haste and awkwardness, but he never did. He often chose a new channel for either entrance or exit, so that a player in my particular position had to be alert to keep from being run over.

Perhaps he found it more convenient to have the risers removed. We now played on a flat stage, which made it easier for our stage manager, Harvey Genereux. But the sound was entirely different. The great sonority of which Koussevitzky had been so proud, influenced by the spaces under the risers, had now disappeared, bringing our sound much nearer that of the French orchestra

Munch had let us hear when he brought his Radio Nationale group to Boston. I felt that we had lost much, but it was not my place to remark on the subject. I yearned for a return of our sound to us.

So we passed our first year and, with the beginning of the second Munch year, we realized that shortly after its beginning we would once more have Koussevitzky with us for a two-week guest appearance. We looked forward to it, of course, if only because some of us were wishing for a return to our older habits of rehearsing, others to make further comparisons and draw their more considered opinions.

During Munch's first year with us, Koussevitzky had gone to Israel, where he had given his organizational abilities to that orchestra, as well as his inspirational gifts to their performances. In the selections that he had chosen for his concerts with us, his genius for program making showed through. His handling of their difficulties only further convinced us that here, indeed, was a conductor of great stature. His program included works by Haydn, Bruckner, Barraud, and Sibelius. It seemed that he had never left, except for the remark from a newer player that convinced Koussevitzky that "now I feel like a guest conductor."

In 1924, Serge Koussevitzky had inherited the Boston Symphony from Pierre Monteux. Monteux went to San Francisco where he developed his great skills and put that orchestra on the map, so to speak. When he reached his seventy-fifth birthday, he voluntarily resigned, although it turned out that he did not mean to retire by any means. He simply wanted freedom to conduct where he wished. So it was that we were to see him during that season of Munch's reign. Of course, we were all well acquainted with his reputation and waited for his appearance with a good deal of anticipation.

In appearance, he could be called roly-poly with justification. He was almost as broad as long, and his height was less than Koussevitzky's. His hair was still black, but his moustache was pure white. He called upon anyone who wished to do so to verify that the color of his hair was genuine. Nature had created this curious combination.

Almost with his first words, he endeared himself to us, at least the string players. After he told us that he was glad to be back after so many years, he requested that the oboe give an A. It was given at such a pitch that he could not accept. He spoke to the oboist and said, "Please, I am an old man and know all the tricks. Now give me the right A!" A note considerably higher was immediately sounded, and we began our rehearsal.

Oboists will, if they can get away with it, give an A lower than usual, so that their own playing is made easier. It took a keen ear to note the difference, and it would appear that he had been subjected to this ruse other times in his career. There was never to be any discussion over Monteux's ability to hear, for it developed that he had a phenomenal ability in that direction.

Playing with this man was a delight. His knowledge of the score; his baton technique, sufficient to indicate everything without saying a word; his authority of what the composer had meant; his years of conducting all the great works of the literature—all combined to bring great joy to those playing with him. That week, we played with him Wagner's "Flying Dutchman Overture," Beethoven's Fourth Symphony, and Stravinsky's *Le sacre du printemps*. This last he had made famous as far back as 1913, when its performance was the cause for a riot in Paris. The program was to convince us that his repertoire was wide ranging. We were to see much of him in the several years to come.

Koussevitzky died on June 4, 1951. We did not mark his passing until the Berkshire Festival season in July, when the full orchestra had come together for our concerts in Tanglewood. At the beginning of Munch's third season, we again took notice of Koussevitzky's death by playing Mozart's *Masonic Funeral Music* on October 5.

Not too long after the beginning of that season, Munch came down with a terrible cold. His doctor instructed him to take certain pills he had prescribed. Munch took one or two, felt so much better that he decided if two were so effective, why not take the others as quickly as he could. There were thirty-six pills in the bottle, and they were of an antibiotic nature. Munch took them at much shorter intervals than his doctor had intended.

We had gone on the road and were assembled to play our concert in Carnegie Hall. While getting ready to step onto the stage, Munch found himself unable to do so. He was rushed to the hospital, and Richard Burgin was forced to step in to conduct the concert. For a time, it was thought that Munch might not recover from this tragic occurrence. Of course, the rumors flew thick and fast. He had been taken by cancer, he had had a shock, he had had a heart attack, etc., etc. Regardless of what had happened, the Boston Symphony was without a leader, and something must be done immediately.

Fortunately, Pierre Monteux was available at the moment, and he was willing to give us two weeks until the emergency could somehow be handled. With music of Bach, Mendelssohn, Hindemith, and Strauss, he managed to fill up his first program, and the second week with some Wagner and Debussy. But he could not stay on, and the management had to fill Munch's place for the concerts that still had to be played.

Thus it was that we were, for the first time, to see Ernest Ansermet of the Suisse Romande Orchestra in Geneva, Switzerland. Ansermet was a man of very distinguished appearance. Bearded, of full height, of unquestioned authority in his understanding of the music he was conducting, he had no difficulty in commanding performances of a very high quality. His programs covered the literature from Haydn, Beethoven, Berlioz, Mozart, Rachmaninoff, and Bartók. He had odd mannerisms, however, particularly that of his habit of beating his chest in rhythm and shouting, "Dug-a-dug-a-dug!" Under Ansermet, with William Primrose as soloist, we performed for the first time in Boston, the Bartók Viola Concerto.

Sir Thomas Beecham arrived to be our guest conductor. Also bearded, also very distinguished, he carried with him that aura that let one know that he saw the humor in music if one wishes to look for it. With him came music for a Handel suite, never before performed in America. We had a rehearsal on a Monday morning that readied us for performance that very evening. On the program, the work was simply entitled, Suite. No indications were given as to its length or movement titles. There were several allegros distributed throughout the music, one of them indicating the tempo of the fourth movement, as well as one that described the speed of the final movement. We were unaware that the printed program failed to differentiate the movements.

With the conclusion of our playing of the fourth movement, a very jolly one, the audience gave us a very warm amount of applause. Sir Thomas acknowledged the applause and asked the orchestra to rise in acceptance of the audience's pleasure. It continued for some time. At last, we could begin to play again. Whereupon Sir Thomas spoke to the audience, "Evidently some of you think we have finished. Unfortunately, we have not. Now we shall play the concluding movement of the suite." Of course, there was a stunned silence, followed by laughter from the audience. A typical Beecham antic!

The next morning as we assembled for rehearsal, we were informed that Sir Thomas had not yet arrived. So we sat until after a half hour had elapsed before someone called the Ritz Carlton to discover that Sir Thomas had not intended coming to the hall at all. Informed that the orchestra awaited his arrival, he rushed to Symphony Hall by taxi and was soon standing before us.

"What is the purpose of this meeting? I thought it went rather well last night, didn't you?" A player spoke up and agreed with Sir Thomas. With that, we heard, "I think in that case we had best go home." We immediately did that very thing. It may be well to look upon an incident of that kind as very amusing, and sometimes very welcome, but it is not the way to keep an orchestra at its peak of performance.

With Beecham's departure, Ansermet returned to us for another two weeks. Until that moment, we had no indication of exactly how Munch might be feeling. Guest conductors had to be the rule for the time. Richard Burgin had one week, Leonard Bernstein conducted us for two weeks, and G. Wallace Woodworth took on the final weeks before Munch's return, for by now it was seen that he could once more take over his duties with the orchestra. He had been away for fourteen weeks. But it was impossible to plunge immediately into a full schedule of rehearsals and concerts. So, the second week of his return, Richard Burgin again took over the baton. Munch came back for the *St. John Passion* the following week; then Pierre Monteux stepped in before Munch finished the season the last of April of that year. Immediately following, we went to Europe for the first time for a succession of triumphant concerts.

The trip was made by boat. We were to have five glorious days of ocean traveling on the *Ile de France*. Boarding it in New York, we were greeted by George Gibbs, past president of the union in Boston, now on Petrillo's staff in New York. He wished us bon voyage, and each member was given a memento to mark our departure.

Late that afternoon, we finally greeted the *Statue of Liberty* on our way from America. We considered it to be an event of a lifetime. The orchestra was grouped in units of four, each unit to occupy one stateroom. It so happened that the group to which I belonged was short one member, and his place was taken by an outsider. We never got to see him from the beginning to the end of the trip, for he got seasick as soon as he stepped aboard and continued so until the end of the trip. His head remained covered the entire trip.

Monteux was a marvelous teller of stories. He beguiled us with his reminiscences as we traveled to Europe. He recalled, for instance, an episode in which he had taken part while he was conducting opera in Dieppe. A new concertmaster had had to be hired, so in due course, Monteux had heard the various aspirants for the position. One chap played better than the others. It was evident, but Monteux noticed that this applicant was a little slow in the wit.

"You know the opera literature?"

"Oui," came the answer.

"Could you begin this evening without rehearsal?"

"Oui."

"The opera we are doing is *Thais*. Do you know the violin solo, the 'Meditation?'"

"Oui."

"All right, you may have the position. But I must warn you that in this theater, when playing the 'Meditation,' the concertmaster must stand up on his chair."

Of course, this was not true, but Monteux felt like indulging his sense of humor. To the amazement of all, when the violin solo had been reached, the new concertmaster began climbing up on his chair. The remainder of the orchestra thought he had gone mad, as did the audience. Monteux stood there grinning, his body shaking in merriment, but he had his joke!

At an earlier time, the touring group that Henri Casadesus had organized was on its way about Europe. The harpsichordist at that early time was Alfredo Casella, a young and hopeful pianist and composer. Casadesus had the habit, when reaching a strange town, of visiting the small shops in the hope that he would discover instruments of such a vintage as would designate them as ancient. In one shop in this town, he came across an old clarinet that seemed to have possibilities. It really did not matter whether or not it was playable. He bought it.

After the concert, as he prepared for bed in the local hotel, he came across the clarinet as he laid out his sleeping clothing. Since the instrument had a reed still attached, he was tempted to try it out, and played a short phrase from the famous French tune, "The Pleasure of Love." Then he merely placed the clarinet in his suitcase and went to bed.

The next morning, as he met Casella, he was questioned, "Henri, I heard a clarinet in the hotel last night. Did you hear it?" Casadesus, an incorrigible joker, feigned a look of disbelief and replied that Casella must indeed be tired. The next night, in another town, Casadesus repeated his playing of the clarinet, knowing that he had piqued the curiosity of Casella. When Casella, now a bit nervous, inquired if he had heard the music, Casadesus, with his most fatherly solicitude assured him that he must be very tired, for he had heard nothing. He went on to recommend a fine doctor in the town to which they were traveling. Casella lost no time in seeing the doctor. His verdict was that Casella had been overworked but that within a few days should be rested enough to return to normal.

That night they were traveling instead of staying in the town, and they were to be berthed in a compartment for four. Casadesus and Casella were not to be separated. Casadesus idled away his time until he could find an opportunity for playing again on the clarinet.

Finally, Casella took his toilet articles and went off down the corridor to the small lavatory that served the car. When Casadesus knew that Casella was behind the lavatory door, he removed the clarinet from his suitcase, tip-toed down the corridor, and prepared to play "The Pleasure of Love" just outside the lavatory door. About to blow the first note, to his surprise the door opened and there stood Casella, staring him in the eye.

Our instruments were stowed below decks. Most of us visited them each day in order to keep ourselves in some state of practice. What a cacophony greeted anyone who stepped in the holds while we were at our practice. No two people in the same key, not even in the same rhythms! After a day or two, Monteux conducted us in an impromptu program, an attempt to entertain other passengers as well as to keep us at a concert pitch, so to speak.

But as all good things must come to an end, we finally reached Le Havre. We arrived very early one morning. There was an intervening period before we should be ready for transportation to our hotels. Some of the members, finding an excellent restaurant right there on the dock, decided to have a bit of breakfast. One of our players, accompanied by his wife, ordered the continental breakfast for both of them. Thinking to make the breakfast a bit more palatable, he called the waiter and in his best high-school French ordered "deux burre," and was surprised to find them being served two beers.

Calling the waiter again and informing him that an error had been made, he discovered the waiter was very willing to correct the error by bringing them ten eggs. Our player finally gave it up as a bad job.

As we moved about through Europe, we came to fully realize just how democratic Munch was. Traveling by day, in the compartments that might house as many as six or eight players, we could find Munch with the card players, totally immersed in a bridge game or the pastime called ballotte. He would even remove his shoes while playing in order to insure complete comfort. How could we have ever imagined Koussevitzky behaving like that! Not for Munch a special car in which he could ride alone. Certainly none of us had to fear meeting him at any time. He was not the taskmaster Koussevitzky had been. Munch did not carry grudges or hold memories of a slip a player might have made last week or recently.

There were to be two big moments in this tour. One was the return of Munch to Strasbourg, his home town and the one in which he had been concertmaster of the local orchestra. It was sort of a home-town-boy-makes-good story.

The big work that would signal his return was Berlioz's *Symphonie Fantastique*. Some weeks before, in anticipation of this tour, the Boston Symphony had procured, through a special order, two bells that would be used in the last movement of the symphony. These bells had cost $5,000 each and were very accurately tuned to the notes they were to play. They were beautiful indeed! We had played the Berlioz work all along our way, and there had been no flaws in our performance thus far.

Playing these bells, a new member of the percussion section had done a most creditable job. The performance moved along, until we had reached the final movement, all well and in good control. The moment arrived for the bell sequence. To our horror, and certainly Munch's, the first bell struck was the wrong one. The second likewise was then heard. Unable to correct his error because of the placement of the bells, the percussionist continued to strike them, to the consternation of all, while Munch shouted, the audience roared with laughter, and the orchestra doubled up in combined surprise, glee, and attempts to keep going. From that time, Munch was to call the offending percussionist "enfant terrible."

On a distinctly higher plane, the second of two incidents stands out. In 1913, Monteux had conducted the *Le sacre du printemps* of Stravinsky in Paris, and a riot had ensued. This would be Monteux's first return with the same work, right in the hall where the riot had occurred. During our appearances before this, we had performed *Le sacre* often under Monteux. Not one performance had been free from a blemish of one kind or another, either that of a mistake by the conductor or from the orchestra. For this performance, we were on our mettle, truly. With Stravinsky in the hall to hear us play, we must give of our best. And we did. Not one tiny mistake was heard during the entire performance!

When it had come to its end, Stravinsky was called to the stage. With tears on both sides, conductor and composer met in a most heart-warming greeting. Players of the orchestra were seen to be in tears, recognizing that we had just taken part in a musical moment that could never come again. Monteux spoke to the audience and reminded them that they had just witnessed his return after thirty-nine years, and that he would vow to return in another thirty-nine years to repeat his performance. He had cause to be proud, but then, so had we!

Our last concert of that tour was given in London. We then went to Southampton to board the *Ile de France* for our return home.

Shortly after the season of 1952-1953 began, we were notified that we were to embark on another long tour. This would be in our own country and would occur as soon as the season had reached its conclusion. Once again, we would have Pierre Monteux as our collaborator, spelling Munch on occasion. The season progressed, and we found ourselves conducted by not only Richard Burgin, but Darius Milhaud, Guido Cantelli, and our old friend Monteux.

During midseason, we were treated to a performance that could not have been anticipated. The orchestra rather shared its opinion of Berlioz's music. What we had known of it had not endeared it to us. Cheap and tawdry did it seem! Facing a performance of his *Romeo and Juliet* did not engender any particular enthusiasm. Very probably more of the same. But to our great surprise, the real Munch was revealed to us. Here was the finest exponent of this music we were to see.

We had done selections from this music with Koussevitzky and even with Bernstein, but when seen in true perspective, their performances paled. I found myself sitting upright in my chair, seemingly above it, with my hair on end as Jennie Tourel sang parts of it. She was the assisting artist who literally transported us into another era with the beauty of her performance.

During the trip abroad, I had amused myself by taking pictures with a stereo camera I had bought for the occasion. I had never been one who took pictures for any reason but to mark the passing of some event in my life. But stereo was something different. Figures seemed to stand out, and color gave them a life that black and white could not have. I had shown some of them around after our return and was complimented on my choice of subject material.

Now facing the 1953 tour in my own country, I was surprised to be asked if I could operate a news camera. I declined the honor, but was invited to do it in a very serious way by Laning Humphrey of our publicity department. Laning and I share no ancestors to my knowledge, but we always found ourselves in sympathy on many subjects, and his invitation was accompanied by suggestions as to how the job might be done.

Eventually, I found myself considering the task very seriously. At Laning's suggestion, I borrowed a Speed Graphic 4x5 news camera and learned how to operate it. When the time came for our trip, I thought myself as well prepared as could be in such a short time. Certainly, I was to find myself with plenty of subject material.

We left Boston on a Sunday night and, within one or two days, were far from our homes and tracking through the Midwest. I sent my pictures—undeveloped—back to Laning in Symphony Hall, and he saw to the rest of it. Imagine my surprise to discover one of my earliest attempts in *Time Magazine*. I had no ambitions to be a press photographer or any other kind. I had to consider how strange life turns out to be. Another with greater ambitions in this direction might have given his eyeteeth for an opportunity to be printed in *Time*. I continued to furnish Symphony Hall with my output and was to act in the same capacity during two other major tours. Eventually, I had seven one-man shows of pictures I had taken for the Boston Symphony Orchestra.

Monteux had his wife Doris with him, but in addition they insisted on having their French poodle, Fifi, as their companion. In our special train, the state room that Karl Zeise and I shared was exactly next to that of the Monteuxes. The porter who saw to our comforts was named Bill. As the Monteuxes would leave for a concert each evening, Bill was expected to watch over Fifi, whose temper was not of the best. After a few days on the road, learning of Fifi's loyalty to her master and wondering how Bill might have learned to cope with it, I asked Bill how he got along with her. To my question, he replied, "Mr. Humphrey, after that door closes on me and Fifi, no one knows what goes on between us."

All my photographic equipment was kept in my stateroom. My viola was kept in the orchestra trunk, which would be delivered to the hall in which our concert would take place. One night in San Francisco, the Monteuxes presented Bill with a ticket to the concert. It was an excellent seat, rather down front, from which Bill could see all of us easily. As I met him back in the train, he surprised me by saying, "I didn't know you could play. I thought you were a photographer." Of course, he had never seen me with anything but a camera in my hand.

We reached New Orleans. Our train was parked in the railroad yards, for we were to be there four days. The Monteuxes checked into their hotel. When they were informed that no dogs were allowed, they checked right out, returned to the railroad yards and their stateroom where they lived during our stay in the city. They really loved Fifi!

Living in a special train gives one far more opportunity to explore the cities one visits. Time does not have to be given to taxiing to the hotel selected and waiting in line for registration. One can immediately begin his sightseeing if he wishes to. And time can be saved on the other end, for after finding one's berth or stateroom for the night, it does not matter when the train may pull out.

We visited many states on that trip and managed to see the most important points of every city on our itinerary. We reached the coast eventually, I shooting away with my camera as we went. San Francisco and Los Angeles gave us warm receptions, as did Fresno and Santa Barbara. Few important cities missed our visit.

Coming back east, we stopped in Salt Lake City, and from there we could visit the huge copper mines of the area. Outside of Denver, we could visit Central City, with its *Face on the Barroom Floor*, as well as its delightful little opera house. Though the tour was made in the springtime, we were caught in a snowstorm in the upper reaches of Central City. I doubt that I shall ever forget the sight of the Golden Gate. And swimming in the Great Salt Lake was an experience not given to everyone.

In the season of 1954-1955, we were given ample opportunity to enjoy the works of Hector Berlioz under Charles Munch. The man was simply phenomenal! Good as he might be in anything else he might conduct, he came into his full powers when treating the music of his great countryman.

In quick order, we were to repeat *Romeo and Juliet* and were to go on to a performance of *The Damnation of Faust*. Here the performance of Martial Singher stood out. There was perfect collaboration between conductor and soloist, equally as good as that between Munch and Jennie Tourel.

Added to this feast of Berlioz, we had a performance of his *L'Enfance du Christ*. None of these works had been performed in Boston, save for a few isolated examples drawn from them, performances that had done little to change the composite opinion of the players. Now Berlioz stood revealed in his greatness through the ministrations of his loving fellow musician and countryman.

In addition to our usual conductors, Munch and Monteux, we were introduced to Ferenc Fricsay. Guido Cantelli also returned for a one-week stay.

Perhaps an event that was not immediately seen to be so important was the resignation of George E. Judd, our manager. He had reached the age of sixty-eight and, although hale and hearty, felt the time had come when he should step down. He had been, as Henry Cabot put it, "one of the most astute men I have ever known." He was a splendid manager of the Boston Symphony Orchestra. Looking somewhat like Munch, the two men had struck up a very warm friendship and were often seen together.

From a beginning when he did not wish to hire me because of the budget of the orchestra, through the years of the union trouble with Petrillo, we had become good friends, and I thought his resignation was premature. He was to live on for nearly twenty years more. We were to see him in Tanglewood through the years.

At some point, we had made the acquaintance of Danny Kaye, known for his work as an actor, humorist, and comedian. Anything which he touched was done in a thoroughly capable manner. Through the intervention of Harry Dickson, a member of our orchestra, it was arranged that Danny should conduct us in an effort to raise money to help offset the deficit under which any great orchestra always suffers.

He came to us as a completely unknown quantity, but it was only a few moments before we recognized his great talents. His conducting showed him to be a person with great rhythmic gifts, as well as a feeling for the humor or the serious aspects of the works he was using. He injected a bit of nonsense into his program with us, to the point where the orchestra hugely enjoyed his antics and was willing to share in the nonsense.

At one moment, he looked up at Munch, sitting in the balcony and sharing our audience's enjoyment, and addressed him as "Chuck," all in good fun. It was a tremendously profitable experience for all, from a musical standpoint as well as a financial one. His final moments were given to sitting on the edge of the stage and having a heart-to-heart talk with our audience. He was to repeat his appearance with us at long intervals.

So taken with Danny Kaye were we and so grateful for his assistance in raising funds for the orchestra that we voted him an honorary membership in our Pension Institution. It was not at all uncommon, when Danny was in the Boston vicinity during later years, to find him pouring coffee for us during our intermission periods downstairs in our coffee room.

As the years passed, Munch had grown terribly lazy and untidy in rehearsal. He expected us to respond to his thoughts, it almost seemed. He did not wish to spend the time to tell us what was in his mind. Rehearsals were shortened, sometimes to a ridiculous degree. Others were canceled entirely. Repeats had disappeared from everything we performed (thank goodness). There were instances on the road when a train had to be caught, when his tempo would be increased to a point where it was almost literally impossible to play the notes required. But we always made the train.

We had added concerts to our season. We had also added, at his suggestion, the open rehearsals, designed only to bring in money. Everything had already been prepared so that our open rehearsals were simply play-throughs of the week's program. Occasionally, the necessity of playing these open rehearsals would appear to be chores that he would rather not do, but they were at his suggestion in the first place.

"Pas necessaire" became the watchword. He had not lost his ability to conduct a splendid concert. He could, if he wished, play the Pathétique magnificently, but he did not love the work as had Koussevitzky. He thought this music unclean and often said so. And he was being troubled by a physical condition for which he had found no cure. He was to remark that the scientists could find ways of doing impossible things, but they could not take care of his condition. It was not to kill him, but it did add much discomfort during those years. How much his life was affected by the passing of his wife, we never knew. During their marriage, they had lived their separate lives, she in Paris, he in America.

We were still seeing Guido Cantelli and Monteux, but now we were to meet Igor Markevitch. He was noted for his rendition of Stravinsky's, *Le sacre du printemps*. He did it well and showed himself to be a very fine musician in anything else he conducted.

The fall of 1955 saw the passing of Olin Downes, famous critic of the *New York Times*. We played Mozart's *Masonic Funeral Music* in his memory. Shortly thereafter, Arthur Honegger died, and we played an excerpt from his own music in his honor.

Finally, in December of that year, Arthur Fiedler got his chance to conduct the Boston Symphony. Koussevitzky's threat to keep him from conducting this larger orchestra had held good through all those years. Munch, having no grudge to settle and being of such a kindly nature, had seen no reason why Arthur should not be allowed to have his chance.

Ansermet was to return for a two-week stay and shared the conductor's duties with G. Wallace Woodworth, Bernstein, and Heitor Villa-Lobos, in addition to Monteux, who, though older as each year passed, gave no sign that his powers had diminished.

In the spring of 1955, E. Power Biggs, the organist, wished to make a tour of Iceland to play concerts on the organs existing in that country. He needed supporting players, and it was decided that he would take a small group with him for those appearances.

But during the stay up there, the orchestra players would be expected to be involved in additional musical activities. Several were to be booked to perform concertos with the national orchestra in Reykjavík, and certain others would form a string quartet that would perform programs in outlying communities.

I received an invitation to be one of the performers, an offer that I eagerly accepted. In May of that year, we set off for Reykjavík. We were fortunate in the weather and that we could enjoy a part of the six-month daylight period of the area.

Small though Iceland may be, it still is an important spot on the globe, lying as it does between Russia and America. Russia had been wooing the Icelanders with all sorts of unusual attractions, from trade fairs to splendid performances of theater and concert programs. To make a fine impression, they had been giving these attractions to the Icelanders without admission fees.

Our American ambassador, one Mr. Muccio, felt that this was the wrong approach since the Icelanders are a very independent people. He suggested that we charge a minimum fee, such as 25¢ in our money and see what would happen. We saw very quickly. We were besieged to the point where each of our concerts was sold out, a very different result from the Russian giveaway of their attractions.

Several of us appeared as soloists with their national orchestra. Emil Kornsand and I performed Mozart's *Sinfonia concertante*, Roger Voisin, Haydn's Trumpet Concerto, and Louis Speyer, an oboe concerto. In addition, the string quartet was active in playing programs. We moved about a great deal and were able to appear in Akureyri, at the northern part of the country, as well as the Westmann Islands, quite a distance from Reykjavík.

So successful were these programs that our State Department felt they should be repeated, so upon our return, we began planning for our next visit to Iceland. Biggs would not be able to accompany us because of previous commitments. This necessitated a change in the personnel. In the spring of 1956, there were eleven of us in the group. The group's members included a clarinet, piano, trombone, trumpet, horn, oboe, and bass that would, like the string quartet, perform chamber music.

We played our first concert in the capital city of Reykjavík, after which six of us went in an easterly direction, the other five taking themselves to the west. We would eventually meet in the little town of Húsavik, the northernmost community of Iceland, only fifteen miles below the Arctic Circle, thus only fifteen hundred miles from the North Pole.

Our meeting place in Húsavik was the little wooden Lutheran church in the center of town. Iceland has neither trees nor shrubs, thus no wood available for building. To find a wooden church in a community so far removed from any source of supply could be considered a tribute to those who had imported every bit of wood to be found in the structure. But another memorable moment was to be enacted.

After the speech of welcome from the local bailiff, a group of men formed themselves on the small stage and sang, of all things, "Kentucky Babe," in Icelandic! We could not understand one word of what they were singing, but the tune we knew only too well, and I think the gooseflesh that formed on my body may be explained. After our concert, we were invited to take refreshments at the home of the minister, some few hundred yards from the church. There we were astonished to be greeted by the minister's wife, smoking a cigar. It seemed the thing to do there.

We were scheduled to play again in the Westmann Islands after our return to Reykjavík, our tour having still some days to run. Westmann is a very small group of islands, served by airplanes that must have certain winds to allow them to land or take off.

When the moment for our departure came, we were told that it would be impossible that day to make the trip. So Karl Zeise and I got in touch with the orchestra's concertmaster and assistant and suggested we play quartets just to while away the time. So enjoyable was this session that we regretted its end. But the next day, our trip to Westmann was again put off, so we returned to our delightful informal quartet sessions. Again on the third day we played together, for the winds were still from the wrong direction. But now our time had run out, and we must return.

We all agreed that we wished to play again, somewhere, and as we made the trip homeward, I felt that I should like to do everything possible for it to become a reality. At the same time, the thought had occurred to me that it would be a wonderful form of collaboration if we could set into motion an exchange that would allow players from each orchestra to spend a season with colleagues elsewhere. The original dream that I entertained would, of course, include players from a string quartet.

I made a trip to Washington and sketched out a plan that would allow two of us to return to Iceland and join with our Icelandic colleagues in a tour of that country. As so often happens, governmental red tape was to interfere to the point that such a journey did not appear feasible during 1957, but we were assured that the plan would go through later, and so it did, in 1958. We returned, Karl Zeise and I, joined with our Icelandic friends, and after sufficient rehearsal time, made the first tour of its kind for Icelandic audiences.

Unbelievably, each concert was attended by a good 90 percent of the town's populations, an unheard-of proportion if we transfer it to our own shores. We gave fifteen concerts in eighteen days. Having been so successful in my planning, I had the audacity to contemplate a still bigger venture.

I hied myself to Washington once more, sketched out an idea for them that, to my surprise, they immediately accepted. Once more, I was able to plan for the next venture. I had in mind the idea that now the Icelanders would visit our country, and in our concert making, our scene of operations would be that part of the United States that had seen Icelandic immigrants settling themselves in areas that would later become thriving and important communities. This would include the two Dakotas, Minnesota, and Wisconsin. I was very agreeably surprised when a gentleman, James Lombard, stepped forward to arrange such a tour and underwrite the expenses involving promotion, program printing, etc. Mr. Lombard's efforts were to smooth our way in innumerable instances.

Karl Zeise, our cellist, was also a watercolorist of some accomplishment. With such a tour in preparation, he was further inspired to make a series of watercolors of Iceland from sketches and memories gathered during a previous trip. So he produced some forty scenes that would accompany us as we toured. Twenty would be sent to our first location, twenty to the second, the first set moving on to our third stopping place, the second to our fourth, etc. This turned out to be a most fortunate idea and attracted much attention, with the result that at the end of the tour, Karl sent them all to Iceland, to be sold for the benefit of talented young artists in Iceland, the unsold to be given to the local museum in Reykjavík.

So, in the spring of 1959, the Icelanders arrived. We used ten days for rehearsals, during the while they lived in my home. Our first appearance was at the Harvard Musical Association rooms here in Boston. Then we opened our official tour in New York City. With those concerts behind us, we moved on to Duluth, Minnesota, and were soon well into our playing in the Icelandic-American communities. As I recall, we gave fifteen concerts in eighteen days, the same as in Iceland, all of which were well received.

In several instances, halls that had been chosen for our appearances turned out to be far too small, and we had an audience on the stage, as well as distributed around the walls as standees. We moved by Volkswagen bus, one that I had purchased at the suggestion of the State Department. It had been agreed that I should receive from the government the amount it would have taken to travel by bus or railroad. I was to pay all expenses during the tour and be reimbursed at tour's end. It was all well thought out and would have been satisfactory, but during the tour and with the coming of the fiscal year's end, changes had happened within our own State Department. When we returned about June 28 or so, I learned that rules had been modified, the older agreements now having disappeared or been forgotten due to the changes within the department itself. I ended up having to pay out of my own pocket the sum of $800.

Still, having reached a certain momentum during the planning of these unusual tours, I had the temerity to visualize something still bigger. I visited the State Department and sketched a plan to them, one that they felt had merit. This tour would bring the Icelanders and Americans together in Reykjavík, there to rehearse until we should be ready to go off to Europe, and finally Russia. We would ask the Soviet Union to furnish one of their excellent pianists for the tour, and we would feature the Shostakovich Quintet as our most important work.

Our government, in this case, agreed to provide protection as we moved about, but could not agree to pay for the venture. They did not feel that America could offer such a tour to the Soviets under existing conditions. Perhaps I could find backers to underwrite the expenses. I was informed that at that very moment, the Soviet Minister of Culture was in New York City, and I could have an opportunity to sketch my plan to him.

I asked for an appointment with him, and we then met together with an interpreter, for neither of us spoke the language of the other. I told him of my hope, my plans to seek funds for the tour, at which he leaped to his feet and shouted something that was translated as, "That is a noble gesture, but we cannot permit anyone but the Soviet Union to pay for such." Having received assurance from him the idea would be accepted, I returned to Boston and saw my friend, Mark Horblitt, a retired attorney of some means.

He thought the venture could be underwritten by him and friends, and asked for a tentative estimate of what such a journey would cost. After some consideration, I suggested the sum of $25,000 as adequate. With that, Horblitt said I should go ahead with my plans. So I did.

I eventually learned that the Icelanders would be given leaves of absence for the tour and ascertained that our orchestra would allow us to be free. In our minds, the young pianist, Ashkenazy, was the perfect player since he was already appearing in America, and we could possibly find time to rehearse with him previous to the tour.

But in May 1960, our U2 flew over Russia and was shot down. Any disclaimers as to its reason for flying over enemy territory were of no avail, and its pilot, Francis Gary Powers, was thrown into jail in Russia, and the incident attracted worldwide publicity. The State Department informed me that in view of this deplorable incident, now was not the time to undertake the tour I had in mind. So it had to be forgotten.

In 1956, the Boston Symphony took off for a tour that would take us through a great part of Europe, but find us in Russia as well. We would be the first symphony orchestra to visit this forbidden country. The tour was to begin in Cork, Ireland. The orchestra was given a choice of traveling together to Cork or of preceding the larger group and using one week's time in seeing Ireland. My wife and I elected to do the latter.

We arrived in Shannon, bused up to Limerick, where we rented a small car and were on our way to a most pleasant eight days or so. We were able to see very well that part of Ireland before we were required to join the orchestra in Cork.

In Dublin, we had the opportunity to see the location where Handel's *Messiah* had been given its first performance. We saw where the king and queen sat, noted the disparity between the placing of their chairs, and could imagine the moment when the king rose to his feet to greet the playing of the "Hallelujah Chorus."

By way of Sweden, Norway, and Denmark, we reached Finland. There we were to be picked up by Soviet planes and deposited in Leningrad. But to our consternation, we were informed that the planes were not available, and we would have to travel by sea to our next destination. But this was impossible if we were to keep to our schedule. Our management found itself up against a stone wall when the subject was taken up with the Soviet officials.

In this impasse, someone thought of putting the problem up to our New York trustee Mr. C. D. Jackson. In a few hours, we received the news that our U.S. Air Force would pick us up and deposit us in Leningrad. With that assurance, the Soviets suddenly found planes that would bear us thither. But such planes! Each held but eighteen passengers, were unequipped with seat belts, had no parachutes, and were completely free of any sound-proofing material. Pilots insisted on taking off without warm-up periods. When landing in Leningrad, we were suddenly brought down in steep dives from whatever altitude. We never knew whether or not we were being given such treatment to show us their skill or to scare us out of our wits.

We were met by a delegation headed by David Oistrakh, Russia's greatest violinist. In due time, we were all housed in the Hotel Europa, not far from the Leningrad Conservatory. From the moment of our arrival, we were approached by one or another persons with offers to buy our shoes. Shoes seemed to be a status symbol. Wherever we went, we were under scrutiny, particularly our shoes, perhaps in an attempt to discover our own standing in our native country. To accede to these invitations to sell our shoes would have been fatal, for we were to discover later that we were under constant surveillance by little men who seldom made themselves evident, but were nevertheless observing us, in order that no untoward incidents might mar our visit.

We were instructed that we might take as many pictures as we cared to. Buses holding eighteen passengers (same as their planes) were put at our disposal. Accompanied by one or another of the interpreters who had joined our company, a bus would proceed at a very fast pace to a park where we would find a statue of Lenin or Stalin in prominent display. We rather disconcerted our interpreter, for upon arrival at a destination, we would leave the bus and scatter for any pictures we might care to make. She violently disagreed with this and tried to insist on our going in pairs. She lost on each occasion.

Finally, once again on board the bus, we would be hurried to our next destination at such a speed that picture taking was out of the question. Another park would be shown us with the same two heroes in statue form on view. It was not long before we recognized that the invitation to take pictures meant nothing. Conditions made it rather impossible!

Karl Zeise and I were sharing a room in the hotel. It happened to be on the second floor, a corner room overlooking Nevsky Prospekt. One was immediately reminded of the days of the archdukes before World War I when one looked at its furnishings. It even had a grand piano as part of its décor. It was the first night of our occupancy that I was awakened from a sound sleep by Karl. He asked me if I could hear a peculiar noise and wondered what it was. It seemed to be coming from outside. We looked out our window and were amazed to see throngs of people on the streets below. It was 2:00 a.m.! These people simply passed one another with no signs of greeting. No smiles could be seen as they passed under the street lights.

We learned the next day that in Russia there were only beds for one-third of the people. A man worked eight hours, slept eight hours, and sat in the park for the remainder of the time. These poor folks preferred walking to sitting in the park, where even a word might be misconstrued. Far better to walk and speak to no one.

I believe it was on our second day in Leningrad that the stupidity of our photographic expeditions finally got to me. Keeping my eyes open as to where we had gone, I informed a fellow player that I thought I would walk back to the hotel and asked him to tell the driver to go on without me. Left alone, I began walking in the direction I thought was the right one. I soon found that I had miscalculated my position. I returned to my starting point and tried three other directions only to discover that I was really lost! Back in my starting place, a park of some beauty, I sat down and tried to think my way out of the situation.

My passport had been collected upon our arrival at our hotel. We had no consulate in Leningrad to which I might turn. Telephones were few and hard to find. I had no money with which to make any call I might have intended, and to make it worse, I had completely forgotten the name of the hotel where my belongings were waiting for me. That turned out to be a temporary loss of memory, thank goodness.

I knew no Russian. My French and German would hardly serve me in case I got a chance to use it. But I decided to try out the only solution I could imagine. Watching the people who passed me, all seemingly in uniform, I picked out a person who looked more German than the rest. In halting German, I asked him if he could direct me to the Hotel Europa. The word, "hotel," seemed to have no meaning to him. I made signs which meant I ate and slept there, whereupon he explained, "gazin."

With that, he made a speech to the assemblage, which by now included some forty or more persons, most of them with smiles on their faces. From the back of the crowd came an answer to his question, and a young lady stepped forward. She told me, in English, that she was a student at the university, was going in my direction, and would be glad to show me the way home. With much waving of hands, I made my departure, and with the young lady, set off down Nevsky Prospekt. It turned out that I was but two or three blocks away from my hotel, and the moment came when she pointed that I should go "down that street." I thanked her and went off in the direction she had indicated—only to discover that she had been in error.

Now, with some experience behind me, I looked for someone with a raincoat somewhat like the one I was wearing and soon discovered one on a chap only a few yards from where I stood. I was very relieved to find him an Englishman, and the language barrier no longer existed. He told me that the girl was almost right, that I was but one block away from my hotel. I thanked him and was soon in what almost felt like home.

Concerts in Leningrad were extremely successful. The applause was loud and long. We learned of a new way to accept it. After what we thought sufficient time, we simply left the stage, and the conductor continued to make his bows on an empty stage to the audience still in full attendance. Although our audience was made up of people dressed in anything but what could be called formal—blue shirts and everyday suits—it appeared to be a perceptive audience. Impassive in their facial expressions, nevertheless the applause was overwhelming in its intensity. We concluded that applause is an impersonal way of saying what is in your mind, that hands may be clapped without changing facial expressions, and no one can prove that you are thinking thoughts contrary to what is expected of you.

About our third day in Leningrad, the Soviets, according to prearrangement, gave our management an amount of money to be distributed to the orchestra. It amounted to about thirty-seven rubles, the ruble being, at that time, about equal to twenty-five cents in our money. It was immediately given to us.

Several hours later, a like amount was brought for the same purpose. Our management protested that the Soviets had already fulfilled their contract and turned the money away. When the Soviets insisted, and implied that our management did not understand fully, the money was accepted and again distributed to the members of the orchestra.

Several hours later, a delegation appeared to ask for the return of the money. They finally admitted that a mistake had been made. Our management informed them that the money had been distributed, and that it would be impossible to have it returned. Much of it had already been spent on telephone messages from Leningrad to Boston.

We were housed in the hotel at no expense to us, our meals were provided, and we were bused back and forth, so that there was nothing we could do with the money but call America!

Later, during a bus ride, some of our members were exchanging news of home, as learned through various wives back in America. One happened to wonder out loud how all those calls had been carried and mentioned that the oceanic cables must have been very busy. Our interpreter joined in the conversation with the question of what was meant by oceanic cables. She would not believe what was told her—that there were about a half dozen cables in constant use, the first of them having been laid as far back as 1889. She looked at us as though we were trying to fill her mind with foolishness.

Of course, we were to learn that the telephone had been invented by a Russian, as had the telegraph and wireless, etc., etc. The largest outdoor stadium in the world stood in Russia and held one hundred thousand people. Holding faithfully to our instructions from our State Department, we did not tell her that we had a stadium in the small town of Ann Arbor, which already held 103,000 and was soon to be enlarged to accommodate 110,000. But it was difficult to withhold such information.

We had been surrounded before and after our concerts by Russian musicians, curious to see these instruments we were using. None of them had seen, for example, a double horn. I cannot forget the moment when the first trumpet of the Leningrad Orchestra was shown the seven mouthpieces and five trumpets used by Roger Voisin. He was astonished that Roger was able to change from one instrument to another depending upon what he might have to perform. He himself was held to the one trumpet and a single mouthpiece!

But the time came for us to move on. Our next stop would be Moscow. We were driven to the train station for an overnight ride in sleeping cars somewhat similar to the couchettes we knew in France.

Having some moments before train time, I remembered that I had promised a friend back home to send him a postcard from somewhere along my route. The choice was very small—Lenin or Stalin pictures were everywhere to be seen—and with little time I was unable to look beyond the displays right there in the station. I bought a card of Lenin, wrote on it, then looked about to find a postal station where I could find a stamp.

At that moment, a little man in a long black coat touched me on the arm and signaled that I was to follow him. I did so, noting that we were going in the direction of a long line of people waiting at the postal window. As we approached, he barked an order, and immediately the line of people moved aside. He took me directly to the window, at which stood a lady buying a stamp. She stepped aside while the clerk was handing her the stamp she had just purchased. I took her by the shoulder and put her back in her proper place, and she received her stamp. I tried to argue, without a word of Russian, to explain that I did not want to displace these folks but when I turned around, the little man had disappeared. There was nothing left to do but receive the stamp necessary for my card and pay for it with what small change I had.

Early the next morning, about five o'clock, we drew into the rail yards of Moscow. Already we could see workers, women mostly, moving rails, oiling switches, and digging holes for some reason. We passed what seemed miles of such activity until at last we had arrived in the main station. We were whisked to the Hotel Metropole, a very new hostelry not yet completed.

As we were given our rooms, some of our members decided to find out if their rooms were bugged. In one case, they exclaimed that "there was no soap in the bathroom" or "they haven't put towels here yet" or anything else that occurred to them. It was only a few minutes before a maid came running with the missing articles, putting our minds to rest on that score. But we noted that in this brand-new hotel, already the plaster was falling from the walls and certain fixtures were nonoperative.

In one hilarious example, the hopper had been placed in the doorway of the bathroom, making it necessary to walk around this important fixture before one could wash one's face. Privacy was out of the question, seemingly.

Again we were regimented to a degree. All meals had to be eaten at the same time, and we were transported, as before, in buses holding eighteen people. Why that particular number of people, I never learned. There was a moment when we were instructed that we would be picked up in about forty-five minutes for a tour. Our interpreters were entirely new to us, we having left our other group behind in Leningrad.

As we heard our instructions, the head interpreter said that there must be no wandering about "as you did," this directed at me. I could only realize how fast news travels and under what scrutiny we had been. We came down for our lunch on one occasion. As we sat there, we heard the tinkle of a glass, and when the speaker had our attention, she informed us that four members had not eaten their breakfasts. We could not be served our lunch until those four had had their breakfasts.

With that, waiters filed in with the four breakfast servings and placed them in front of our four colleagues. We broke into rather angry urgings to the offending players to hurry and finish, so that we could eat lunch. When they had finished, lunches were brought to all, including those who had just had breakfast. Regimentation!

GUM was a revelation to us. GUM is the largest mercantile emporium in Moscow. To purchase anything displayed, one had to line up and pay for the article still to be purchased. With the receipt in one's hand, one then made one's way back to the counter that held the article to be purchased, and if it was still there, complete the transaction. In more that one instance, the delay caused by the prepayment could have allowed another to have purchased it. I purchased a Russian bear carved out of some native wood, a bottle of Star of Moscow perfume, and a small silver tea-glass holder. With that, my seventy-five or so rubles were almost gone. I had but four left.

Our concerts were, as before, extremely successful. Our audiences overwhelmed us with applause. Once more it became necessary for the orchestra to leave the stage while the conductor continued to take the applause from an empty stage.

As an added gesture of friendship or statesmanship, whichever, we were offered an opportunity to visit the mausoleum where the bodies of both Lenin and Stalin were to be seen. We were transported to Red Square, there to see a long line, four abreast, lined up for what was about a half mile, all waiting to visit this shrine. As our party approached the entrance to the mausoleum, the folks about to enter were instructed to step to one side, and our party was allowed to precede them. This was a grisly moment, indeed. There lay Lenin, and beside him Stalin. Lenin looked as though he were masked with some lifelike material, Stalin as though he had just been out for a walk and could rise up and speak to us!

We were later told by one of our English consular attachés, who accompanied us on the whole tour, that Stalin still required his moustache to be trimmed, that his hair continued to grow. We were not allowed to take pictures, and the movement of the line precluded any stopping for better views. In a few moments, we were through the Mausoleum and into the clear air of Red Square. How ghoulish to consider that all these people waiting their turns had only this sort of thing to worship.

That night, after our concert, we were given a grand sendoff. At a party thrown in our honor, we found Khachaturian, Kabalevsky, and Shostakovich, as well as other important people in the Soviet hierarchy in attendance. It was only natural that our retiring hour was rather late.

Our room in the Metropole was furnished in what I can only describe as undertaker's décor. Huge drapes crossed each window; our beds with their huge canopies were draped in velvet that closed off the occupant. From our window, we could see the red star that showed us the location of the Kremlin.

We were to depart the next morning. Because of that strange number of eighteen still being in effect, we were taken one group at a time to the airport. Karl's group was to leave at 2:00 a.m., mine not until 6:00 a.m. Karl offered to tiptoe out and leave the door unlatched, so that I should not be awakened. I vetoed this idea, for I knew that sleep was impossible for me once he had left. I much preferred to get up and lock the door. The memory of those two dead faces, the sight of the red star, our funereal room furnishings made me only intent on locking the room as soon as I might. Karl left; I locked my door and waited.

At five o'clock, I was already packed, sitting in the lobby, ready to go. At six, we filed into our bus and were about to take off when one of our interpreters came rushing out of the hotel. She shouted, "You cannot go. There is a brush missing from room 605." This at 6:00 a.m.! With that, we waited until she finally came to tell us it was perfectly all right to depart. We, however, refused to move until we should be told who took the brush. She informed us that it had been taken by a member of a Bulgarian delegation, and with that we were on our way.

We had been told that we would be given breakfast at the airport before our plane was to depart, but upon arriving at the airport, we were ushered into a waiting room from which we were expected to board our plane. We were then told that because we were already late, breakfast must be forgotten. This did not fit with us, and we simply staged a sit-down strike until we should be fed. For some reason, the arguments became my responsibility to answer, perhaps because I was very adamant about our right to have the promised breakfasts.

Finally, we were asked what we wished. The reply was "orange juice, eggs, toast, and coffee." We were told that they would be provided.

We had some time to stroll about the airport, and I remembered the four rubles still in my pocket. I would not be permitted to take them out of the country, so I decided to buy a bar of chocolate with them. I selected one and gave the counter lady my four rubles. With that, the lady raised her voice and began shouting as though I had tried to rob her. I found that the cost of the chocolate bar was twenty-nine rubles, more than six dollars in our money. I handed the bar back, took back my rubles, and looked about for the next best solution. A gentleman passing by became the repository for my rubles, for I simply dropped them into his open pocket. Perhaps he is still serving time in Siberia for possessing more than his share of rubles.

Eventually, we were informed that our breakfasts were prepared. Of course, we should have known better than to ask for orange juice. Instead, we were served a drink we had already learned to call "Seven Down." Identical omelets had been made for us, some toast, and the inevitable *chai* (tea) took the place of our requested coffee.

Once aboard our small plane with eighteen seats, we could only do as they planned with us. After four hours in the air, we came down in Vilna, Lithuania, where we were met by officials of the airport. To our surprise, we were ushered into a room where we were to eat our breakfasts. It was now 12:00 o'clock noon, some four hours since we had eaten.

To our surprise, we found the identical place setting we had seen in Moscow. Of course, we were hungry enough to do justice to the Seven Down, omelets, toast, and *chai*. Once fed, we took to the air again and were deposited in Vienna before the day had finished. Anxious as I had been to visit Russia, I was far more anxious to leave it. The experience, however, was worth anything we had been through.

Reading over what I have already written, it would seem that during Munch's time, we simply traveled and had no time at home. This is not true, for there was a full schedule of concerts back in Boston. As a matter of fact, we continued to add more concerts to our already heavy schedule. But much of the travel I and several others of the orchestra participated in was of our own doing. The two trips to Iceland and the eventual tour of the Icelandic-American quartet were not required of us, but something we did partly to escape the boredom of always playing the symphonic literature, partly from a desire to assist in the State Department's plans, and partly to spread the gospel of chamber music wherever we could.

In 1960, our orchestra was designated as the one that should visit Japan and other parts of Asia. The trip would take us as far as Australia and New Zealand. Once again, I was named official photographer for the trip. We took off with much fanfare, stopped for a short while in San Francisco, then proceeded to Hawaii, where we spent about two hours in the airport, and then proceeded on our way. We landed in Tokyo, but without even deplaning, we were off to Taipei, which would be our first official stop.

As we landed in Taipei, we got our first glimpses of the water buffalo used in their farming activities. A caribou-like animal, it is used in the many aspects of agriculture, as well as a general beast of burden. The weather was foul, and it became a slogging match to arrive at one place after leaving another.

We were taken to our "hotels," each of which bore a name somewhat fanciful in content. The group to which I was attached was housed in what was called Blue

Heaven. We tried to spend as much time as possible in the Officers' Club, for it was quite a bit homier than our little hotel. But it was a bus ride of a somewhat long distance, and to stand about in the rain and wait for the bus that would take us there was not an enjoyable way to spend the day.

Our hotel was seemingly open all night. At any moment, we found ourselves descended upon by girls who would sit on the edges of our beds and ply us with questions. "How many children have you?" "Do you have a wife?" or "My name is Peggy. I have three children." This at 2:00 a.m. They would be wide awake; we hardly awake enough to answer their questions. They might sit there for a half hour or so. It was only at checkout time some three days later that we got an inkling of what was going on. The lady at the desk took hold of my hand and nuzzled it in a most affectionate manner. Then she revealed that her establishment was something other than a hotel. It had been taken over, drafted as it were, to house that portion of the 122 men in our party. She had agreed to suspend all other activities while we were there.

We swung back to Tokyo, to be used as our headquarters while we played our many concerts in Japan. We were housed in the Daiichi Hotel, in the Shimbashi area. Some thirty days would be necessary for us to complete our Japanese part of the tour. Some quaint memories come to mind. In the lobby of the hotel sat ten or a dozen little girls, all uniformed in the hotel's colors. They responded to any necessary calls and seemed to be in motion continually. We could hear, during the night, the sound of an oboelike instrument and the faint cry of a man's voice. He turned out to be the noodle man in his rounds during the night. His function was to provide sustenance of a kind for late travelers. The sounds of the little bus attendants as they blew their whistles as signals for the bus drivers are not to be forgotten.

We noted the attempts of Japanese girls to dye their hair red to conform to our Western appearances and thought it rather deplorable that they should make the attempt. The East, as we saw it, had a charm that could only be erased if they persisted in their attempts.

So to and from the Daiichi we went, often to towns or cities that lay at some distance from Tokyo. We were continually amazed at the fine acoustics of their concert halls. It turned out that NHK, comparable to our own NBC, had erected these halls with acoustics foremost in their planning. In most cases, they at least had been successful.

We moved about Japan under the traveling aegis of JTB, the Japan Travel Bureau, growing increasingly tired. We found the Japanese inns, charming though they were, to have bedding material totally unsuitable to our needs. We slept on the floor, on mats always too short for the occupant. But then we learned that there were Western hotels along our route, and we found that the Western hotels were being occupied by the Japanese Travel Bureau employees seeing us through the tour, while we were given what they thought we would most enjoy. We put some pressure on them and were finally able to use the Western hotels ourselves before we one and all collapsed from sheer fatigue.

One of the loveliest memories of our concerts in Japan is that of those moments after a concert was finished. Munch would come back to the stage for his second bow and several little girls would come out to meet him. They would be dressed in their kimonos and would have bouquets of flowers in their arms. Very prettily they would shyly present the flowers to Munch. Munch would then re-present them to someone in the orchestra whom he thought had played particularly well. I don't believe we played one concert in our whole tour when this formality was not observed.

After we had played in Sapporo, the site of a famous university, we were invited to attend a seminar of young people. In my capacity as photographer, I had a double reason for being there. In company with eleven other players, I lined myself up on the stage in front of perhaps one hundred students who directed questions at us through an interpreter. Each of us had to answer, as best he could, the question directed at him. I don't remember what my question was, but I evidently fielded it to the satisfaction of all. After this question and answer period, we all mingled in a tea taking for a few moments.

While I was having my cookie and tea, the interpreter stepped up with a man of about forty-five in tow. The interpreter asked me to accept a gift from the other chap. It turned out to be a fossil shell in the form of a snail. It was explained to me that this gentleman had been carrying it since he was about eight years old. I was told that it was a piece of ammonite, some eighty million years old.

It was further explained that when in doubt, my new friend touched this fossil, which was always carried in his trouser pocket. As he touched it, he was reminded of his own insignificance, he said, and that the answers to his inner questions would sometimes come to him.

I was very embarrassed at the gift and asked what he would do now since he no longer had his amulet. He said he would find another fossil of similar age and continue his practice. I could not refuse his gift, of course, and accepted it with the greatest thanks I could give through our interpreter. I still have it, and must admit that there are times, when appearing in a solo capacity, I find myself reaching for the little fossil that I also sometimes carry in my own trouser pocket.

At one point, we set out from Kobe for a boat trip across the Inland Sea, our destination being Beppu. As we left Kobe, we saw a group of young Japanese girls, all in uniform. We learned that they were off on holiday and returning to the mission they attended in Beppu. In some manner, we learned that they had not slept the night before. Having been given a berth for myself on the boat, and having no use for it, really, I asked one of the girls to use it, and she went off to bed.

The trip was a long one, during which we saw patrolling submarines and one or two other strange sights. Eventually, the girls' group regained its usual daytime wakefulness. They let us know they wished to sing for us and, when we made no objection, obliged with a group of choral hymns of a Protestant nature. My little sleepy friend turned out to have the loveliest voice of all. She led the group in everything they sang. So entranced were we by her personality and obvious excellence of voice that we hoped we could help her in furthering her singing career.

Back in Boston, I investigated the necessary red tape one had to go through for having her pursue a career in this country. I was told that I had to give information as to her scholastic accomplishments to date. I wrote to her requesting her record. It never came, but we did receive at Christmas time a tape of her singing Christmas carols, in English! We never heard from her again.

It was while we were touring in Japan that someone came across an announcement of a movie that depicted the sinking of the *Ile de France*, this beautiful ship of such fond memories. Several of us were very interested in seeing the movie and one day started out to do so.

No one who spoke Japanese among us, we could only write down the name of the theatre and its general location, and then try to find it. Coming into the area that we had learned contained the theatre, we accosted a gentleman who appeared to be of a friendly nature. When we had showed him what we had written, he invited us through sign language to follow him. Down the street we went, around this corner and that, until we had progressed a distance of six city blocks. By this time, we had become embarrassed at having caused him so much trouble, but there was nothing we could say to deter him from his kindly mission.

Eventually, we reached our destination. Our friend pointed it out and then started back over the route we had just traveled. We had interrupted him in one of his more important errands, I am sure. Our thanks had to be given in sign language, of course. We were to discover that to be the Japanese way of helping one lost in their country.

The *Ile de France*, coming to its end, had been bought by a Japanese company to be cut up for junk. Learning of its availability, one of the Japanese movie makers hit upon the idea of making a movie using the act of sinking the ship as the theme of the movie. It was towed to the Inland Sea, and a location was chosen that would allow the ship to sink almost completely, but not quite so. When the movie had been completed, the ship was raised and towed to its final resting place. Viewing the movie brought back many memories to those of us who saw it.

Earthquakes are daily affairs in Japan, we had been told. We could expect them at any moment, they would cause little trouble, etc., etc. It was in Dogo that we had our first encounter with this new experience. As we sat on our floor waiting for breakfast, the house began to shake and creak. Mindful of what we had been told, we cautioned each other not to exhibit the fear we actually felt. My wife, Karl Zeise, and I were in the little group that so assured each other.

As the shaking began, the little maid had been in the act of entering with our breakfasts. She set the trays down, fell to her face, and began to moan. We learned later that, although she was Japanese, this was the first quake she had lived through since becoming an employee of this inn. The tremor soon passed, and we had our breakfasts immediately. We had not been aware of the real danger that we had so blithely disregarded.

As we arrived in Dogo, students from a nearby university had offered their services to us. Two who attached themselves to us were name Cato and Utsonomiya. Everywhere we went, they followed and were indeed of great help as we traveled to this location or that. They spoke English to an extent and felt this a splendid opportunity to further their English knowledge.

A group of us had been exploring the delights of this little spa when lunchtime came. We came upon a small restaurant and after some examination of the food articles displayed behind glass outside we decided to have the following: soup, sandwich, ice cream, and coffee. We waited politely and soon the coffee arrived. Soon after, the ice cream was brought in. Having finished with them, the sandwiches appeared and eventually the soup. All were exactly in the reverse order! Perhaps there was a reason for this living in reverse, but up to now, I have never discovered it.

We had grown very fond of our Japanese companions. We had seen them almost constantly for three days. Now our time was up, and we must move on. As the afternoon of our last day was upon us, the two boys asked if they could go to our room so that they could just talk to us. Once there, they unburdened themselves of the many questions still to be answered. It was a very heartwarming session, I can tell you.

When we had answered everything they had asked, I proceeded to unburden myself of a thought that had been in my head. I put it thusly, "In 1945, with the dropping of the atom bombs on Hiroshima and Nagasaki, some of your relatives must have been killed or horribly maimed. You yourselves are hardly able to remember the incident, but some of your relatives must still feel that we are your enemies. With such knowledge in your heads, how are you able to treat us as you have, with certainly great kindness and no exhibition of hate?"

Their answer was very simple, "We believe that what has gone on before is past. We do not know what is coming, so we have only the present time in which to live."

Further questioning revealed that they do not worship a god as we know him, but a force that may be called nature or the Creator. Not even the teachings of Shinto or Buddha can alter their reliance on their beliefs.

I had to admit that with their philosophy, as they explained it to us, they had reached a higher level of understanding than many persons I knew back home who were professed Christians, but only lived their beliefs on Sunday when they attend church.

We left by boat the next morning. Almost as our boat pulled out, we were conscious of a bicyclist in a great hurry to reach the boat. It turned out to be Utsonomiya, who had pedaled seven miles just to say good-bye! We had only a moment or two before we had to part from him.

Leaving Japan, we went on to Manila. In frightfully hot and damp weather, we tried to do our best musically, but it was not easy at all, broken strings and long bow hair making it difficult in the extreme for the string players to perform well. It was so hot during the day that it was very uncomfortable to walk on the streets.

We were warned that a stroll during evening should not be considered, so unsafe would it be. It was not uncommon for several knifings to be reported each morning. Still, we managed to get about and see certain worthwhile sights. We visited Taygaytay, some miles north of Manila, and had lunch overlooking the huge crater that marked the position of the dead volcano. We were able to see the only bamboo organ in the world.

We viewed the aftermath of a huge tornado that had passed only a few days before. We watched people diving into the inky waters, looking for possessions that had been torn from them in the disaster. People dispossessed by the tornado had to seek refuge in the local cemetery, where they could sleep on the gravestones that covered the resting place of one already gone on. We viewed a cemetery that housed the remains of American soldiers killed in the recent war with the Japanese.

It was only a short time after our return home that we read of the so-called dead volcano's coming to life, causing a catastrophe that completely destroyed the area and took a good many lives with it. So sudden was it that it could as easily have occurred as we sat quietly having our lunch.

With our arrival in Australia, we could enjoy the climate of a semitropical country. The winter we were to experience when we returned to Boston could be deferred, if only for a short period. It was very delightful. Brisbane, Sydney, Melbourne, and Adelaide—all were our stopping places.

I recall an incident in Adelaide. As I came down to have my breakfast, I was guided by the hostess to a table already seating three persons. In our country, I would have been given a table by myself. As we approached the table, I could very well see the jollity they were showing. Two men and a woman were already seated.

With my coming, faces assumed a very serious look. No word of greeting was extended, and in silence I looked at the menu and finally gave my order. I asked for orange juice, scrambled eggs, toast, and coffee. As I pronounced my choice, one of the men spoke up and said, "Ah, an American, eh!"

"How did you know," I asked.

"No one could pronounce 'scrambled' as you did unless he was an American," said he, as he screwed up his face and made to imitate my pronunciation.

"Well," I replied, "I am sure that if you appeared in Oxford, England, no one would have difficulty in judging you an Australian. We don't speak the language. We use it in various ways."

I went on to explain that none of us would be able to read Chaucer as it was written, so many changes have crept into the language we share. There was no offense intended, and we continued to talk in quite a friendly manner until we had left the table.

In Sydney, we had time to visit the local zoo, of wide fame, and got our first views of the duck-billed platypuses, emus, and koala bears in their native habitat, as well as a few other strange creatures to be seen only in such a zoo. Our concerts were very successful, but we experienced a difficulty we had not expected. Due to the change of seasons, it had been thought best to turn off heat in the concert halls. As a result, we played one or two concerts in our topcoats over our full dress. Even so, we were able to do a creditable job.

We moved on to New Zealand, still enjoying the warmth of a tropical climate. We played in Auckland and Wellington, and then it became time for us to return to Boston. My wife had elected to skip New Zealand, and instead she went to the Fiji Islands where she enjoyed a week of an entirely different kind of life. We returned to America, she scheduling herself to leave Fiji at about the time we should arrive there. Our arrival in Boston thus coincided within a few hours.

The orchestra immediately plunged into a full symphony schedule, even though we were all suffering somewhat from what has come to be called jetlag.

Shortly after the completion of our Asian tour, the orchestra was asked to assemble in our tuning room. Munch and Henry Cabot, our president of the board of trustees, greeted us and divulged that Munch had decided to resign after the next season. He had reached, said Cabot, the age of 70, had found the increasingly hard schedule to be very taxing, and wished to leave the orchestra while he was still able to conduct elsewhere. He would be succeeded by Eric Leinsdorf.

Viewing it in retrospect, the thirteen years of Munch's conductorship had been productive of many new things for our orchestra. Our repertoire was much augmented by more French music than we had been used to playing. Many of these works had been done by Koussevitzky through the years, but with Munch they became our more usual fare. The exclusion of Tchaikovsky's music (except now and then) had allowed the music of Berlioz to be given its full due. But we never knew what we might be called upon to do, so inspirational was this man. A very splendid concert one day might be followed on the next by one that had very little to recommend it, even though the program might be exactly the same.

We made recordings, the like of which could not have been even thought of during Koussevitzky's time. The technique of recording had advanced to that point. It was still difficult but possible. One in particular comes to mind. We recorded the Berlioz Requiem, which requires, in addition to a full orchestra, a full chorus and four bands.

So huge an undertaking did this appear that critics and other musical representatives from New York made a special trip to Boston to observe the proceedings. The orchestra sat on the floor of Symphony Hall, all seats having been removed for the occasion. The chorus was seated on the stage, while the four bands were distributed to four corners of the balconies.

With his special gifts, Munch was able to coordinate these far-flung groups into an acceptable whole, and the recording resulting was indeed a formidable one. He had a flamboyance about him. His conceptions were large, though lacking in detail, and it was impossible to fail to recognize his stature as a fine artist in anything he did.

Admittedly, he was lazy. He did not like rehearsals, but then, neither did the orchestra. But rehearsals are necessary, and it is just as well to recognize the fact. After rehearsals of minute details by Koussevitzky, the almost negligible attention Munch gave to these same works could not but affect our rendition of them. Still, the personnel of the orchestra had remained somewhat as Koussevitzky had left it, and the memory of our earlier performances with him kept us playing better than Munch might ask for.

In his final season, Munch selected guest conductors who would take from him some of the load, not that he would rest. He would be off conducting somewhere else. Richard Burgin, Ernest Ansermet, Steinberg (our first glimpse of this newcomer to our orchestra), Guilini, Carvalho, and even Nadia Boulanger. Munch closed out his career in Boston with a performance of Beethoven's Ninth. We would see him again only as a guest conductor. And we knew we should not see his equal again. We genuinely hated to see him go.

CHAPTER 4

The Later Years

Erich Leinsdorf

Having spent fifteen years with Koussevitzky with his detailed rehearsals, his insistence on color in the sounds produced, and his complete dedication to the task at hand, I had formed the belief that this was the way a symphony orchestra should always sound. This was not a question I had given much thought to. We had simply always sounded that way, and I thought of our sounds as completely natural and expected of such a body of players.

Without doubt, Koussevitzky's baton technique left us often without full knowledge of exactly what he meant, and I had cherished the wish that someday we might have a conductor who would more clearly indicate the progress of a phrase without glossing over the measures and leaving us without clear indications of his intentions. I often wished that we would complete the measure we were playing without having to jump to the next measure prematurely.

So we got Munch, and I expected that much of our troubles would be over. Not at all. We simply had more of the same thing! A wave of the baton would be all that we saw. It was up to us to fill in with what should be in between. In moments of conductorial inspiration or improvisation, the baton might reach the next beat before we had caught up with it, indicating a new tempo depending on the conductor's whim. So we had not gained in that respect.

We had lost any reason to mold our tones to fit the work we were doing. Since Koussevitzky, we had never been asked to do so. So we had lost that art. The attempts at balancing the sections were almost nil, the conductor's intention seeming to be the larger picture to be drawn from the work. Much as we had grown to love Munch, we could not be unaware of the qualities that he did not have. He had no patience for the small niceties of music we might be playing; he was untidy in rehearsal and so anxious to get through this chore that he left much undone, expecting us to remember from past performances what to do, to call upon our techniques to produce results not even rehearsed. It was indeed time for a change, especially since it was his wish.

Yet he left us a legacy that none of us would ever be able to forget. His performances of anything written by Hector Berlioz were sublime. He brought to that music the result that the composer must have heard in his mind when he composed it. He had shown kindness in his treatment of the players. We truly felt a great loss with his leaving.

Almost with the announcement of Munch's leaving, and that his place was to be taken by Erich Leinsdorf, we were conscious of our new conductor. In the procession of guest conductors that passed before our eyes after the announcement of Munch's leaving, we had seen him February of 1961 when his program had included music by Richard Strauss, Dallapiccola, Shubert, Wagner, and Brahms. In this country, his experience had been with the Rochester and Cleveland orchestras, plus some conducting at the Metropolitan Opera.

Unquestionably, he was a conductor of some technical stature. But now we were to see him almost continually, and he hadn't even taken over his new position. Munch had been Musical Director of the Berkshire Musical Festival as well as the Boston Symphony, but in reality he left the musical festival in the hands of others. But already during the Tanglewood season of 1961, we could find Leinsdorf on hand. It became a joke of a kind, which tempted certain people to rename him Erich U. Leinsdorf, the U standing for ubiquitous or underfoot. He was already giving instructions for changes in the library, changes in the artists' room, and in his own to-be conductor's room, etc., etc. Little escaped his eagle eye.

But it was not until the beginning of the 1962 season that he began his official duties with us. It was at once evident that he was indeed on top of the job. So well did he know the music he was to conduct that he dispensed with the scores during performance. This in itself is no sign of musicianship, for a conductor may be able to recall every little indication the composer has put into his score, yet that same conductor may not have any indication of what the composer really intended. So much of music has to do with emotions felt, the same way in which our spoken word may indicate inner feelings by the way it is inflected.

Still, he exhibited every indication of a well-equipped conductor. His arms were somewhat long for his body. He could reach far out over the orchestra, it seemed. Not that that was any point in itself. Our memory of Pierre Monteux was of his short arms. But what he could do with them!

Leinsdorf had a very disconcerting habit, that of conducting without a baton. Any man may lose a baton at times and be forced to go on without one. We had seen it happen to both Koussevitzky and Munch. But to do it deliberately was outside our experience. The baton is a sort of extension of the arm, be it short or long, and it serves to give an exact point that will indicate the beat more exactly than does the hand alone.

To make it more difficult for us, he kept his hand somewhat clenched with no extended finger to give us any kind of a point. In contrast, the batonless Stowkowski used his index finger to serve as a point. Of course, the player can become accustomed to this rather vague way of indicating musical desires, but only accepts it because he can do little else.

The net result was that we were playing with a lack of the incisiveness sometimes necessary for clean performance. But this did have the result of removing from our performances the woodenness of the conceptions of our new conductor.

When he stepped on the stage for our first rehearsal, he did not come as a stranger. We had already seen so much of him before he took over the job that the impact of his arrival was somehow lost. He gave the impression that he meant to be the conductor and boss in every way.

He let us know that rehearsals would be put on a schedule of so many minutes for this and so many for that. This was a completely new way of rehearsing for us. We were not used to a conductor's being able to tell a choir of players exactly when they must be on the stage to play. Neither Koussevitzky nor Munch would have been able to forecast the progress of any rehearsal they might have held. But Leinsdorf seemed to wish to work that way.

Koussevitzky's dress during rehearsal was impeccable. He was turned out in an almost elegant manner. Munch, much less conscious of his appearance than Koussevitzky, nevertheless still made a very neat and presentable figure. To our amazement, Leinsdorf came to rehearsal dressed in a sweat shirt! He was very clean about his appearance but to appear in that attire did not seem to us fitting! Yet he continued to dress that way all during the time he was with us.

Leinsdorf had soon committed to memory the name of every player. He did have an extraordinary memory, one had to admit. And he soon began to make efforts to bring himself closer to our players. He would invite small groups to have lunch with him to get better acquainted. Little was to be gained by this endeavor, however. The players of a symphony orchestra are not in the habit of hobnobbing with its conductor, certainly in Boston, so his cultivation of us fell on sterile ground.

He was married to a lovely lady, one who was a sister of David Sarnoff, president of RCA. There was a suspicion that he had been chosen for more than his musicianship. Was not RCA our recording company, and were we not very closely tied to them in a business way? Was it not expected that record sales and concert attendance would increase to the joy of all?

Early in his work, we became aware of his extraordinary knowledge of the languages. His native tongue had been German, yet he was completely at home in French, Italian, and of course, the language of this country. A truly well-educated person, without doubt. But he began interjecting certain words so frequently that we grew weary of hearing them. His favorite seemed to be "juxtaposition," and after that "relay." He used these continually in explaining what he wished of us. Eventually, it became our habit to make a noise after the use of either word, and eventually he caught our message to him and gave up their use.

He also had taken on another habit that became very irritating to all of us. Just moments before a concert's beginning, players (solo mostly) would find new instructions on their stands as to how they should play in certain places. In some instances, a whole section might receive instructions in this same manner. We were not accustomed to this treatment and, in fact, rather resented it.

In contrast to Munch, who usually dispensed with repeats to the joy of our players, Leinsdorf seemed to be of the exact opposite belief. He took them religiously, even to the point of adding one here or there according to his wish.

I recall one performance of Mozart's *Jupiter* Symphony to which was added a repeat of the last movement. The time of playing that symphony thus became forty-six minutes, the usual length of a Brahms symphony, we having already taken all the repeats originally written. Somewhere he had absorbed the belief that concerts should be at least two hours long. Perhaps that explained his penchant for repeats. They were certainly time fillers. But Koussevitzky had given concerts that were often but one hour and forty minutes long, a much better length, thought most of us.

The audiences had been very enthusiastic, and we had not grown too tired to throw our best efforts into what we were doing. But almost religiously, Leinsdorf stuck to the two-hour length! Often we would play a considerable time after we thought we should be through. We could see the people heading for the doors long before we had come to the end of the program. This should not be, for I feel a concert should be designed for the pleasure of the audience.

Although Leinsdorf was completely in command of any work we might be playing, we began to feel that his heart was really wrapped up in works that utilized the services of choruses or came closer to being something of operatic origin. The frequency with which we found choruses sharing the performance with us was greater than we had known heretofore. It is only a short time until an orchestra wearies of this practice and loses a great deal of interest that they might have otherwise retained.

Leinsdorf's programs stayed pretty close to the Teutonic literature. He was, however, enterprising enough to play many a work new to us, and we began to see music of Benjamin Britten, Etler, Fine, Kirschner, and Lee, to name but a few—all composers save Britten, of secondary stature. He failed to include some of the French literature to which we had become accustomed. It was, therefore, very pleasant to welcome Charles Munch as a guest conductor, who returned us to the world of Fauré, Ravel, Franck, Ibert, Honegger, Berlioz, and Saint-Saëns all within a space of three weeks. A bit later in that season, we were conducted by Pierre Monteux, who gave us an opportunity to play some Debussy, Beethoven, and Hindemith.

At the end of that season of 1962-1963, we made our second transcontinental tour, this time with Leinsdorf. It was done mostly by plane. No longer did we have time to become acquainted with any of the cities or towns in which we played. After the concerts, we were taken to our hotels, picked up in midmorning, and whisked to the airport for a trip that might consume several hours. Arrival in a new area was usually at such a late afternoon hour that we had no opportunity to stroll about before sundown and our concerts. It was a much more hurried existence.

The same schedule would be repeated the next day. What had been a pleasant experience in earlier years now began to approach the nature of a chore, and it was a relief to return to Boston.

In late 1961, I had suffered an automobile accident that left me with a whiplash injury. I had a recital coming up in March of 1962, a program for viola and piano of contemporary music for the combination. It was necessary to postpone the concert for a month, but with the coming of April 1962, and with the help of a mechanical gadget I had made at MIT, I was able to play the program and also continue my work with the Boston Symphony. But it was very hard going. As the months rolled by, I began to lose the ability to raise my arms.

As the summer of 1963 approached, I was aware that something had to be done, and very quickly if I was to continue in my profession. Consultation with an orthopedic surgeon at Massachusetts General Hospital had not been too edifying. The only thing that he would advise was an operation that, if unsuccessful, would leave me paralyzed from the neck down. He informed me that even he would not have such an operation. I was scheduled to enter the hospital during that September for further examination. My surgeon suggested that I go to Tanglewood, play what little I could, and rest for the ordeal I might have to face in the Fall. I explained all this to Leinsdorf, who very kindly suggested that I follow the doctor's orders explicitly, and, that if anything happened that would allow me to play again, to feel free to rejoin the orchestra.

I arrived in Tanglewood armed with my cameras, with the idea in mind that I would illustrate a book dealing with Tanglewood and its approaches, physically and mentally. So I started on this new project. As I moved about the village, one after another of the permanent residents inquired why I was wearing a Thomas collar. They regarded me almost as a native, so many years had they seen me about.

I explained my condition to them and each came back with the suggestion that I see a Dr. Brinker of Great Barrington. So insistent were they, and so desperate was I, facing an operation that could take away from me any hope of continuing my career as a musician, that I finally did go to see Dr. Brinker, a chiropractor, one of those people I had been warned against. But his approach was so different that I was soon convinced that just perhaps this man could truly bring me back to a playing life.

Agreeing to lie on his table for a trial adjustment, I was startled to feel, with his first application of the treatment, a snap in the affected area, a snap I heard as well as felt in my body. The pain immediately stopped, and I almost whooped in astonishment and surprise.

Next day, the pain had not returned and I went back to work. Leinsdorf let me be the judge of what I could play, and I spent one hour daily with the orchestra from that time forward. I continued to see Dr. Brinker every other day during my stay.

When I finally returned to Boston and presented myself to the hospital, my surgeon told me that I was cured and did not need to submit to the operation. I hadn't intended to anyway, believing that with proper treatment I would be able to continue my career, which I did for fifteen more years up to my retirement.

I saw Dr. Brinker at intervals, even making the trip up to Great Barrington from Boston on occasion. I feel I owe him and Leinsdorf a large debt for their consideration and understanding.

When Munch returned the next season, he gave a performance of Leonard Bernstein's Symphony no. 3 (*Kaddish*). Before he had departed the next week, we had heard Nicole Henriot Schweitzer in the Ravel Concerto in G.

Several weeks later, we were to have our first experience with Leopold Stowkowski. I had first heard this man during my attendance at Curtis Institute in Philadelphia back in 1930. I had not felt, at that time, any urge ever to play with him, not caring for his general approach to music, his lack of a baton, and many small things I had heard about him. Now, well advanced in years, he had dropped some of the traits I had so deplored, and I could view him much as I could view another guest conductor.

Stowkowski immediately showed himself to be a master of his art. Much as I might not care for what he sometimes did, I had to admit that he indeed knew what he was trying to do and accomplished it very admirably. Still without a baton, he employed his index finger for the smaller indications a musician needs to properly do his job. With a different stable of composers, he gave us a varied program that included not only works by Mozart but Hovhaness and Ned Rorem.

On a subsequent appearance with us in Tanglewood, we were about to begin an open rehearsal when the sound of a crying baby was heard from the far reaches of the Shed. Stokowski immediately remarked, "I didn't do it," but a few moments later, added, "But I wish I had." Still living up to his reputation.

When Koussevitzky had been replaced by Munch, we had found ourselves playing on a flat stage, much to the detriment of what we had considered our sound. Now, Leinsdorf replaced our old risers, but only in part. Such risers as now were used were very shallow and used only in the rear of sections to allow players to see the conductor. The old Koussevitzky sound seemed to be a thing of the past.

Leinsdorf was an excellent pianist, for his earlier training had been as a coach in European opera houses. He seemed to delight in playing the harpsichord in baroque music, and he did an excellent job of it. In conducting accompaniments, he was completely adequate. He certainly knew the score of anything he was doing and was very meticulous when working with the soloist. We never felt at a loss as to what was desired of us.

There was one occasion, however, when we were completely nonplussed. We were in New Brunswick, New Jersey, and were finishing our program with the playing of Dvořák's *New World Symphony*. We had reached a point fifteen measures from the end of the work where a chord of the fifth is played. The chord comes at such a time, and in the midst of harmony, that might cause the listener to believe the work had ended. With its playing, Leinsdorf bent over with his beat, his customary manner of finishing, and remained so. We waited for the rest of the movement. Nothing happened! Minutes seemed to pass, although they were in realty only short moments. Leinsdorf remained in a bowing position, facing us.

Evidently, hearing no applause usually given at a work's end, he suddenly realized that someone had made a mistake, perhaps even himself. With that, he straightened up and gave another beat. The orchestra took up its work and, accompanied by the surprised conductor, brought the symphony to its conclusion. It was but one indication of what can happen when a score is not used. It was never mentioned later.

Somewhere along the line, he had known one of our players, not too happily, it seemed. On occasion, he would revile this player in Italian, the player's own language. The Italian sounds that flew back and forth were not of a friendly nature. We felt for the player, for the conductor is always considered right, no matter what.

With Leinsdorf's accession to the position of our conductor, we were introduced to two men who would be his "assistants." Charles Wilson and Andrew Raeburn were to be found at all times with scores in their hands, sitting at different positions in the first balcony. They would call out, at times, suggestions as to how to balance the orchestra or point out a wrong note here or there, all things that any fine conductor should feel his own responsibility.

Wilson was a conductor who could do a creditable job when given a chance, but his function seemed only to be to balance the sections and to guard against wrong notes. Raeburn's function seemed simply to report on how the orchestra sounded in relation to some recording or other put out by Decca, with which he had once been affiliated. Now we saw the ambition of Koussevitzky completely turned about. In his day, we had tried to play our very best, as in a concert, leaving the recording of our efforts to RCA upstairs.

Now we seemed to be trying to make our orchestral sounds compare to a recording from which Raeburn had drawn his own ideas of how we should sound. It was not too difficult to observe that our individuality was being lost with the passage of each day. We had passed still further from those days of elegant sound, which we had grown to feel was to be expected from a great symphony orchestra.

The days of tape recording had arrived by then, also the days of having sixteen microphones hanging over our heads. We were distributed about the floor of Symphony Hall, each section segregated from the others, but expected to play only with Leinsdorf's beat. He would be the coordinator. We really tried, but such playing is impossible! It is necessary for each player to hear what is going on about him before any kind of ensemble can result.

But recording by tape had made it much simpler to record any of the repertoires of a symphony orchestra, or any group, for that matter. With this method, an error made by a player can be remedied simply by replaying the passage with the correct note added. The offending moment is removed, the corrected one substituted through the expert use of scissors and mending tape, and none can tell the difference. Gone are the days when four and a half minutes of recording on wax might be ruined by an error during that last ten or so seconds.

But we grew so efficient that other aspects of our music making were lost. Very little of a personal nature was to be heard in our playing. Of course, we could perform anything in the symphonic literature. Our players were capable, more capable than they had been in the early years of my membership, but we now sounded less together, less dedicated than in those earlier years. It had to tell in our playing, especially that heard on our records.

In the meantime also, the lesser orchestras of another day had grown into an excellence that could be a competitive factor not to be disregarded. If we recorded the Fifth Symphony of Beethoven, it now had to compete with twenty-five other recordings from all over the globe.

Buyers of recordings had come to expect a recorded result that could not have happened in actual performance. The use of tape precluded that. Seldom is a symphony orchestra heard in concert without errors creeping into its performance. In its recorded performance, none of the clinkers are allowed to remain. For whatever reason, the sale of our recordings began to fall off, no matter that we were the aristocrat of orchestras.

As I have previously mentioned, I had visualized a project that would result in an exchange of players between one orchestra and another. I had thought of some European group. But when I had advanced the idea to our management, I had been told that it was not feasible, and I had dropped the subject.

However, one of our members, George Zazofsky, a first violinist who served as the chairman of our orchestra committee, in looking about for an innovative idea, had come upon the possibility of such an exchange as I had visualized, although we had not worked together on it previously. He thought it up for himself.

By the time it was broached to the orchestra, it was already established that the participating orchestra in such an exchange was to be the Japan Philharmonic Orchestra, one of the six already existing in that largest of the world's cities, Tokyo. I was immediately interested, but I could not apply for inclusion in the exchange. My duties on a research team at MIT called for my presence. I had looked forward with great anticipation to the idea of the exchange, however.

When my duties at MIT were temporarily discontinued because of the incapacity of the leader of the group, I signified my wish to be included, and thus I was released from Boston to join the Japan Philharmonic with the beginning of the 1967 season.

I had been sitting on the third stand of the viola section. Directly ahead of me, Albert Bernard had given notice that he would be retiring with the beginning of the 1967 season. I would automatically replace him. Realizing that many things can happen in such an event, I wished to insure my own promotion to his position.

So I went to Leinsdorf and got his assurance that the position would be mine after my return from Tokyo. I also got a letter from our management to the same effect and breathed much easier after I had accomplished those two tasks. While I was away, my new position would be filled by Jerome Lipson, who would move back into my old position once I had returned.

I studied Japanese during the months preceding my move to Tokyo, but found it an almost impossible language for me to assimilate, that is, for any real use. I learned probably forty phrases and about one hundred words of objects, etc., but found them almost useless when I was actually in that new land, for the phrases I knew were the wrong ones, the objects always ones for which I had not the Japanese equivalents. But I learned while there that I was not alone in my ignorance. According to the writings of Lafcadio Hearn, one of the foremost authors on Japanese subjects, Japanese is a language that can only be properly used by one born and brought up there.

When the idea of such an exchange had become finally agreeable to both orchestras, Leinsdorf had made a trip to Tokyo and listened to the players who were to be selected as the first exchangees. He chose certain of the players interested in the idea and returned to America.

Unfortunately, he also made certain statements that were to follow him and be reprinted, much to the embarrassment of the Japanese orchestra. He classed them as mediocre and went on to compare them with other groups in this country, none of which had any stature in America. However, the exchange was approved, and the first exchangees left us in September of 1966. Robert Karol and Richard Kapuscinski, violist and cellist, remained in Tokyo during the nine months of the orchestra's winter season in America, and then returned for the Tanglewood season of 1967.

I then journeyed to Tokyo, there to assume my new duties with the Japan Philharmonic. With Ronald Knudsen, one of our excellent violinists, we joined with our new colleagues. The concertmaster, Louis Graeler, formerly of New York City, made up the trio of Americans who sat among these Oriental players.

Ron and I had been exchanged for a violinist and a violist. The violist was Akeo Akaboshi, first violist of the orchestra. Although I had not anticipated this, I found myself designated as the new first violist. I declined the honor, however, preferring to sit with my old friend, Konosuke Ono, who had returned to his native land after serving as an exchangee in the first year of 1966.

In the absence of Akoboshi, his stand mate had moved over to assume the duties of first viola. It was immediately apparent that he was not happy in his new position. Still, I had not intended to assume it either, and I felt much more at home on the third stand. We had been told, the two American players, that we would be given an opportunity to be heard in solo works during our stay there. That was well and good, for sufficient time would be allowed us to prepare.

We were already hard at work with our chosen piece, the *Romantic Fantasy* of Arthur Benjamin for violin and viola and orchestra. I have never been able to properly play the incidental solos that fall to the first violist, even though I may know them by heart. The efforts of playing a recital or concerto performance are much more suited to me, for in one or the other appearances I am able to get my full control and play as I know I can.

The orchestra, under Akeo Watanabe, was a good one, well schooled in our Western music. Watanabe, a former music student at Julliard, had returned to his native country, and there he had organized this orchestra twelve years before. Made up of young people at that time, the average age of the players in 1967 was but thirty-two! The digital dexterity of the Oriental players was certainly sufficient. The notes, of course, came out, but the sounds were strange to our ears. We pondered over it more than a little.

I was concerned about my ignorance of the Japanese language, but I need not have worried. The instant the conductor gave an instruction, it was immediately translated for me, and I was at much at home as though I had been there forever. Watanabe himself spoke fine English as well as a very cultured form of Japanese.

I have spoken earlier about the manner in which Koussevitzky played the music of Sibelius. In the years after his retirement, we had played little of this composer's music, but upon those occasions when we did, the net result was rather tame by comparison. No chill winds blew over us as one after another conductor presided over the orchestra.

Only a few weeks after my arrival in Tokyo, the Sibelius First Symphony was programmed. I expected more of the same lukewarm performance I had experienced in Boston. But with the beginning of the work, I began to feel the coldness of the North, to my wonderment and delight. So pleased was I that I could not keep myself from speaking to the conductor of my delight at what we had just done. To my astonishment, he replied, "But Mr. Humphrey, did you not know that I am half Finnish?" His mother had indeed been a full-blooded Finn! Strange how one's birthright will show itself.

The Japanese do not celebrate Christmas as we do, but spend as many as eight days celebrating New Year. At that time, all sins are hopefully atoned for; the new year is to be a better one for them, and it seemed fitting that they should contemplate their good fortune.

I had remained in my position on the third stand with my good friend, Ono, where I felt perfectly content. Masayuki Hayashi continued to lead the section. Watanabe suggested several times that I take over the position, but I declined the offer each time. I had by this time grown quite fond of certain players of our section, but found them unapproachable in a sense.

During the New Year's celebration, a party was given, a practice of the Japanese when there is any excuse for it. The party was held in our rehearsal room at Fiji Television Studios. There, tables were heaped high with good things to eat, and the sake flowed very freely. It so happens that I do not drink alcoholic beverages, but I noticed others who thought differently about them.

As the evening progressed, I saw a quartet of viola players weaving their way toward me. As they reached me, arm in arm for support I am sure, they bowed in unison. The first violist, Hayashi, then spoke to me and told me how glad they were to have me with them. He went on to say they would consider it an honor if I would lead their section, now that I felt more at home. I thanked them for their kind words, but told them I was perfectly happy in my position on the third stand. Hayashi then asked me if I could not agree to lead the section for at least one week. I saw no reason why I should continue to be so standoffish, so to show my good feeling in return, I replied that I would be glad to do that.

With that, he whipped from behind his back a viola part that was to be performed during the next week. I had no intimation of this, but he had, due to his looking over the concerts still to be played. The part was for the solo viola that had to be played in a new work by Toda, a Japanese composer. It was entitled *Concerto grosso*, but I would be required to sit all by myself, removed from the orchestra and play a number of solos. Hayashi had been unable to face the task, and I had foolishly acquiesced!

Still, having given my word, I could hardly renege, and with the next rehearsal, I was sitting in the seat of the first violist. The Toda performance went well, although I do not consider it a work I care to hear frequently. My own participation convinced me that I would be able to do a creditable job were I to continue in the position, so I made known my feelings to all interested, and with that, I became first violist of this very good Japanese orchestra. Hayashi sat beside me, and we became very good friends.

During the first year of the exchange, Robert Karol and Richard Kapuscinski had performed Richard Strauss's *Don Quixote* and elsewhere Mozart's *Sinfonia concertante* had been played very recently. Ron and I felt that we should perform something not previously heard in Tokyo. We had chosen Arthur Benjamin's *Romantic Fantasy*. This is a very difficult work, and we had to spend much time on working out its problems, but we were ready with it at the proper time. We performed it on January 18 of that new year of 1968. The performance went well, we thought, and hearing a taping of it later, we were convinced that we could not have played it much better.

We were to see several guest conductors, most important among them, Igor Markevitch, with whom we performed among other things, the Stravinsky *Le sacre du printemps*. Istvan Kurtesz did the Kodály *Háry János* suite, which gave me another chance to play an important solo.

Markevitch sent for Ron and me. He had learned of the exchange and wondered if it might be instituted between his orchestra, the Madrid Symphony, and the Boston Symphony. He surprised us both by telling Ron to his face that he would not wish him. He wanted only players who had played with Koussevitzky in Boston and would know the bowings that had been in effect at that time. I don't know why he had included Ron in the meeting. But it would have been impossible for a good many reasons, and the question never went further than that mention of it.

A most peculiar experience fell to my lot. Hideo Saito was announced as a guest conductor. All I knew about him was that he was director of Toho University's music department, and that he had been a former pupil of Emanuel Feuermann.

With the beginning of rehearsal, I noticed that his technique was a bit faulty. He seemed to be bearing the weight of the world on his shoulders, and they were heaving in a heavy manner with each beat.

We were doing, among other things, Enescu's *Rhapsody*, a piece that contains a prominent viola solo. I knew the solo from memory and had very often played the work with Arthur Fiedler. As we reached the solo, Saito set a very slow tempo that increased the difficulty of the solo itself. I stopped after a few moments and asked him if we might take it a bit faster. There was a dead silence, to my great surprise. Saito skipped to a point beyond the solo and continued with the *Rhapsody*.

After rehearsal, back in the apartment, I sat and considered the whole incident. I realized several things. First, I was the guest in a strange country, the conductor wished it to be that way, and I was being impolite in questioning his wish. I determined that the next morning I should tell him that I would do my best if he wished it in such a slow tempo.

So the next morning, I entered the rehearsal hall, and catching sight of him, I immediately started toward him. To my great surprise, he also started toward me. We met in the center of the room, and as I began to speak to him, he said, "I have been thinking of what you said, and I will let you play it the way you wish." I replied that I would do anything that he might prefer. Neither of us was angry at this decision.

The moment arrived for the solo to be played. As I started to play, he laid down his baton, and the orchestra accompanied me in my tempo for this solo. Then, to my consternation, the orchestra broke into applause! I could not understand. Later, with rehearsal's end, the members lined up; and as they came to me, they each said something of the same sort, which was "Thank you for what you have done." I was still at a loss to understand their remarks, and it was only after I had spoken to my friend, Ono, that I could understand what they meant.

Saito, during the war, had been relieved of his duties at Toho and been designated as one who should propagandize his people and convince them that Americans were indeed savages, capable of all sorts of atrocities. During those several years, he had come to be called the Iron Man of Japan.

Returning to civilian life, he continued to bear this designation. My words to him, innocent though they may have been, were the first that had been spoken in any criticism of what he might be doing. In the public performance, he repeated his hands-off action and let me play the solo at my own tempo. Perhaps, as I later thought about it, I had caused him to lose face, and he did not want to be held accountable for whatever I might do. We were to meet during the remainder of my stay in Tokyo, both showing a dignity and respect for each other.

As we traveled over Japan, I had to accept the fact that I was a *gaijin*, or foreigner. Though I traveled with the orchestra as a full-fledged member, I was still required to pay more for my room than others. When I questioned the practice in one instance, all I got was a shrug of the shoulders and an explanation that such was the law and nothing could be done about it. So, after a while, I ceased to question the practice.

During the summer, the orchestra took a long vacation, and many members went off to the northerly town of Shio-baro. They spent their off time in the pursuit of chamber music. Both Ron and I were invited to accompany them, all expenses paid. There we were able to coach certain groups as they learned one or another of the works we already knew so well. At the end of our stay, a concert was given. Ron and I were asked to perform also, and in company with Yoko

Hayashi, probably the best violinist among the Japanese, we played the Dvořák Terzetto for Two Violins and Viola. I cannot forget those moments, when, in our bare feet, we stood up and performed the work.

Even at that great distance, we learned that back home, Eric Leinsdorf was coming to the end of his stay with the Boston Symphony Orchestra and would be replaced by William Steinberg. Whatever the reasons, our record sales had fallen off greatly, and many of our subscribers had failed to repurchase their season tickets. I could not but recall the words of Henry Cabot, "We hire them, and we can fire them."

Mildred and I had arrived without furniture, but temporary gifts had seen to our needs. We had rented a very small two-room apartment near Daikanyama Station, within easy distance of my work. It had been the first apartment building erected after the war, the first reinforced concrete in the history of the land. All to follow were of like construction. We had bought two beds for our use.

As our June departure time approached, Ron and I received invitations to stay on for another two months. Back home, the Japanese exchangees were attending the school at Tanglewood, which would occupy them until late in August. They were filling our positions in our Boston orchestra. Both of us agreed. But our wives were scheduled to return to Boston in June, and their traveling depended on certain chartered flights.

We sold our beds, returned all borrowed items, and moved out of our apartments. Both wives returned on their previously scheduled flights. Almost immediately, the Japan Philharmonic Orchestra departed on another of its tours. Upon those occasions when we returned to Tokyo, I took a room in the Fairmont Hotel, a lovely establishment overlooking the castle moat. Our trips were to take us into many hitherto unvisited towns, and we both later congratulated each other that our decision had been the right one.

We had been very sorry to learn of Leinsdorf's fall from grace, as it were. We could not be blamed in any way, but it is not pleasant to witness the downfall of another.

With our return to Boston, Leinsdorf's promise to me was seen to be kept. I assumed my new position with the beginning of the season, and Jerome Lipson moved back to my vacated position. We had returned from Japan only days before Boston's new season began, so it required almost a week before the fourteen-hour difference between the two cities was absorbed, and we could apply ourselves with our full capacities.

That last season with Leinsdorf was little different than the others had been. The same meticulous attention to all we did, the same lack of personal touch to what we performed, and the same excellence in performance, without anything beyond it. But now we had a conductor who seemed to prefer indicating every little phrase of any work we might be playing. We found ourselves constricted in such ways that whatever beauty of treatment we knew the music had gained with another treatment was no longer ours to enjoy. The very thing I had always wished for now became anathema to me, for with this x-ray treatment, all inspirational possibilities had gone. We found ourselves playing woodenly.

Still, Leinsdorf was a master musician and a very intelligent person. He was a born organizer or producer whom we all felt was in the wrong branch of his profession. Little by little, we lost contact with him in our work. It began to tell in our performances, to the point where subscribers fell way. Eventually, our record sales revealed that our performances were no longer considered superior, although Leinsdorf had begun his career with us by causing advertising to be issued that proclaimed us the aristocrat of orchestras.

William Steinberg

When William Steinberg greeted us as he assumed the position as our permanent conductor with the beginning of the 1969-1970 season, he stated that it was his intention to bring the orchestra back to the playing we had done under Koussevitzky. Admittedly, an agreement that we were now below our previous level. Without being pessimistic about what he had just said, those of us who had been around in those very years he was discussing could hardly believe the task possible. Steinberg was certainly not the one to do it. He had none of the qualifications as far as we could see. I felt that the man did not even know, from any experience, what it was that Koussevitzky had or how he got such results from his orchestra.

Time would give Steinberg an opportunity, but nothing we had as yet seen from him led us to believe he could accomplish his intended task. We had been conducted several times before by him, always with the result of giving good concerts, but none of outstanding caliber. Certainly he knew his literature, that of the German composers, but once he stepped outside that Teutonic repertoire, he was lost.

His reputation thus far had been founded on the fact that he was of assistance to Toscanini in founding the NBC Orchestra, which he had had on occasion the opportunity to conduct. Before that, like Leinsdorf, he had gone the rounds of European opera houses as coach and assistant to whoever was officially in charge. He had finally landed a permanent position in Pittsburgh, where he was said to have a lifetime contract. It was soon evident that there lay his heart. Every few weeks, he would be replaced by one guest conductor or another, so that he could continue his work in Pittsburgh. We felt his lack of real interest in the Boston Symphony.

In appearance, Steinberg was not what might be called a handsome figure. Tending toward the obese, his structure was not enough to offset this appearance of portliness. His steps on and off the stage were of very short length, and thus he took more of them, giving the appearance of almost mincing. Such was not really the case, however, for he showed no other uncertainty in his gait.

In rehearsal, his words were few, but delivered in an accent that left no doubt as to the country of his origin. They were well chosen and came from an obviously cultured individual.

His baton technique was not unusual. Often he would conduct in a circular motion, a la Toscanini. At other times he would cease to move even a muscle of his body, trusting us to play the music it was obvious we knew so well. He was generally of a kindly disposition. The times he exhibited anything like a temper during the several years he was with us could have been counted on the fingers of one hand.

He had been at some time or another, according to his own accounting, a violinist in a German orchestra, for he exhibited a knowledge of certain difficult violin passages and occasionally advanced an idea of how they should be solved. It was difficult to imagine one of his build gaining enough violin technique to overcome some of the difficulties violin playing presents. Still, if he said he had been a violinist, it must be so, and he did give good advice on occasion to the string sections of the orchestra.

Due to his age and sick condition, we regarded him as an "interim pastor," one who was simply filling in until another conductor should arrive. How long he would remain, we had no way of knowing. He was still at the same time Music Director of two symphonic groups, Pittsburgh and Boston.

We grew accustomed to prolonged intermissions, periods of time that would allow our conductor to rest for what was to come. It was always obvious that his physical condition was not of the best. We felt for him but also felt that with one full-time position in Pittsburgh, he should not have agreed to conduct in Boston at the same time. To neither could he give his very best, and we were not used to conductors who might use us simply as an adjunct to their more important work elsewhere.

Having grown up, as it were, with the violence, occasionally, of Koussevitzky's conducting, the exuberance and vitality of Munch, the cool but controlled technique of Leinsdorf, the conducting of Steinberg, knowing as it was, was about as uninspiring as it could be. I had lost, a long time since, the yearning for exact indication of every note. Such conducting removes any inspiration coming from the conductor and brings a performance exact in its presentation, but completely bereft of any message to our listening public.

But very often during a concert, we would find ourselves playing without a single movement from the conductor. Was he sick or tired? He would simply stand there while we played, a beatific smile on his face and a twinkle in his eyes, but otherwise showing nothing. We could find little to admire or respond to.

Yet he was a very fine musician. In this respect, he was exactly what we had found in Leinsdorf. But he was a sick man already, and we could sympathize with him.

When we made a European tour in 1971, it had already been announced that he would be succeeded by Seiji Ozawa, the young Japanese conductor. We appeared in Vienna during the tour. Our program would feature the Mahler Seventh Symphony. We knew it from other performances, and Steinberg had known it all his life, I am sure. But not one note of preparation had been played in anticipation of this appearance.

There Steinberg stood, giving little indication of what he wished, while we performed this huge work in the very same hall that had known Mahler and, before him, Brahms. Later, we learned that the musicians of Vienna were laughing at us for having to perform this work. If we had not done it, they would have been required to as an annual chore. The work is a great one, but too much of anything, they felt, becomes enough.

The orchestra was outraged that we should have been so humiliated! Our artistic advisory committee called on our trustees after we had returned to Boston and told them of our feelings about the incident. The trustees were amazed that we should resent it so. The committee went on to say that the orchestra would not play for this conductor any longer. They then learned that Steinberg had been engaged for a six-week guest conductorship during Ozawa's first season. The committee stood its ground and was finally influential in cutting Steinberg's stay with us to two weeks.

How sad to witness the end of a man's career, especially in this peculiar manner. Unquestionably, it had been a mistake for Steinberg to take on the added duties of conducting the Boston Symphony Orchestra when he already was supposedly giving his best to Pittsburgh.

In spite of his fine musicianship, he could not continue as he wished, and any attempt he might have made to return the orchestra to the playing Koussevitzky exacted from us had to be forgotten in the greater need to preserve even enough energy to give us his minimum. Steinberg was almost useless to us as a conductor. A sick man, who had his heart on another love in Pittsburgh, he did what was necessary, nothing more. We felt little from his interpretations and knew, with a sinking feeling, that we were not the orchestra we had been. His programs were good, that is, if we stayed within the boundaries of Teutonic music.

Arthur Fiedler

Back in the very early days of the Boston Symphony Orchestra, it had been the custom for European players in the orchestra, mostly German, to return to their homes with the ending of the symphony season. In some cases, players failed to return, feeling that the money earned here did not allow them to remain for the many weeks of off-season.

The idea was put forward that a shorter season be originated that would keep these players here in Boston. The Promenade concerts, later shortened to Pops, came into being in 1885 and had the desired effect. These Pops concerts were to include music of a much lighter nature and would be conducted by competent musicians, sometimes drawn from the orchestra, or on occasion, from other areas of musical endeavor. The concerts became immensely popular.

In 1927, Alfredo Casella, a famous French musician, was engaged to lead the orchestra, now many years old. His programs were drawn from the best music he knew. Unfortunately, his choice of Strauss's *Till Eulenspiegel* and such were not to the public's fancy, and it began to stay away in droves. Things were at a very low ebb, and something would have to be done to restore these concerts to the public's favor. Casella had been there three years when the trustees asked for his resignation—but without anyone to turn to!

It was at that moment that Arthur Fiedler stepped suddenly into the picture. Fiedler had joined the Boston Symphony sometime in 1915 and proceeded to be active in capacity of a violinist, later a violist, a pianist, and even a percussionist, where he would officiate in whatever capacity he was needed.

With the coming of Koussevitzky, he and Jesus Maria Sanroma were called on by Koussevitzky, in his earlier years, to reproduce on two pianos some of the new scores written at that time, so that Koussevitzky might be able to hear certain aspects of them. Fiedler also played celeste when needed. A very valuable man, indeed.

Arthur asked the trustees for a chance to revive interest in these Pops programs, and the trustees gave him the opportunity. In 1930, he took over as conductor of the Pops orchestra.

Immediately, he created a format for the programs to be heard. He did this by dividing his programs into three parts. The first part would include a fine overture and some very well-known symphonic work known to be a favorite with Pops audiences. The second third would include a performance of a well-known concerto, piano or violin, or other instrument, played by some soloist who was known to be completely capable of playing it well. The last third would include music for the younger generation of arrangements of current Broadway hits.

The new format was immediately successful, so much so that soon it was difficult even to get a ticket for a performance. In addition, Arthur had interested universities, colleges, and certain schools in buying blocks of tickets for a special night that would salute the appearance of one group or another. On occasion, the entire hall would be taken over by a group to commemorate one anniversary or another. Special nights were inaugurated such as Old-Timers' Night, when old hansom cabs would be seen at the entrance to the hall, carrying those swept up by the idea.

Early in my time in the orchestra, we were to give the first performance of Walter Piston's *The Incredible Flutist* with the Jan Veens dancers. Still later, Isadora Duncan's dancers were to appear with us.

In his earlier years, Arthur had been active in playing the accompanist's role in recitals in and around Boston. But he had secretly nursed the ambition to be a conductor. He had organized the Fiedler Sinfonietta and was somewhat active with that group, traveling as far afield as Nova Scotia on more than one occasion. He had eventually taken on the conducting for the Cecilia Society as well as for Boston University. So he was already an experienced conductor when he assumed that role for the Pops orchestra. He continued with these duties during the winter season, as well as giving concerts with the Pops in communities near Boston.

In his capacity as conductor of the Boston University Orchestra, he was always looking for new works to perform. Thus he came upon a work of Vaughan Williams, *Flos Campi*, which would require, in addition to a small orchestra and chorus of twenty-three singers, a viola soloist.

Arthur had played my accompaniment when I played my audition for Koussevitzky, so he knew my playing. I was agreeably surprised, however, when he approached me and asked me if I would appear as soloist with him in the Williams work. Of course, I agreed, and eventually we gave the first performance of this work in America. Still later, I was to appear with him and give the first performance in America of Hindemith's *Trauermusik*, the last written to suitably mark the passing of King George of England.

Arthur continued to be able to play the piano. I recall a Pops concert when the Bach Concerto for Three Pianos was played. With Jesus Maria Sanroma and Heinrich Gebhardt, Arthur appeared in the capacity of third pianist, at the same time conducting the Pops orchestra. Later he was to confine his piano playing to the reading of scores, at which duty he was very assiduous.

Arthur had been a member of the orchestra he was now conducting. Players who had not been his friends when he played could not find it in their capabilities to now accept him as their boss. They did not feel that he was their superior in music making, and it galled them to have to take orders from one who so recently had been simply one of them.

Discipline was very poor as a consequence. And it was a fact that Arthur could not dismiss any player in the orchestra. That right was still in the hands of either Koussevitzky or our management. The Symphony orchestra was still the reason for our existence. The time had not yet come when the Pops orchestra became a moneymaker of great importance. So Arthur could only conduct, feel hampered by the attitudes of his former colleagues, and go on in spite of them.

We were to know those moments, in a far-off land, where the existence of the Boston Symphony Orchestra was almost unknown to the people we met; however, when we mentioned that we also played in the Pops orchestra with Arthur Fiedler, their respect was immediately apparent.

Not so long ago we were playing in Ames, Iowa, the Symphony under William Steinberg, and the Pops orchestra under Arthur Fiedler, for one concert only.

Two townspeople were overheard in a local restaurant. The first said, "I see that you are having Arthur Fiedler this week."

"Yes, he will be conducting, but the work is so hard he had to bring Mr. Steinberg along as his assistant."

From the moment of taking over the conductorship and planning of the Pops concerts, Arthur had decided that we could not play any stock arrangements. One after another, fine arrangers had been hired, those who could take one of the well-known show tunes or any other and orchestrate in such a manner to cause the tune so treated to have a new interest to our audiences. No one else could play these arrangements, for they were made for the Pops orchestra alone. That, in great part, is responsible for the sound of the Pops orchestra, in addition to Arthur's desire for the sort of sound that he felt was best. These arrangers have included Peter Bodge, Jack Mason, and Richard Hayman, the last and the most prolific. Many of the best works were written by Leroy Anderson expressly for the Pops orchestra, and we gave their first performances.

Arthur seemed to love to rehearse. Before we joined the union, it was customary to have eighteen rehearsals during a period of ten weeks, the usual length of the Pops season. Arthur would use every moment of his given time and seem to wish more. He proclaimed himself a "perfectionist" as an excuse for taking so much time over items that would almost correct themselves if left to the players.

No player wishes to make mistakes, and if one should occur, the player usually takes it on himself to correct his error. These errors can be made simply because of faulty manuscript, especially in the case of a new arrangement, for example. The player corrects the note at the moment or makes a sign that it should have been this or that, and the second time does not make the same mistake.

It is, therefore, very galling to the orchestra or the player involved to have the conductor make a big thing of the incident and go over it time after time to ensure correctness in another playing. This we resented, for Arthur seemed to have no faith in the players serving him.

But with our joining the union, we decided to define what we considered a necessary amount of rehearsal. We had to perform every evening, and rehearsals are time consuming as well as energy users.

We suggested twelve rehearsals per season, Arthur holding out for the usual eighteen. We finally compromised, after bitter words, at fifteen, each to last only 2 ½ hours.

Concerts were also to be shortened from three hours to two and one-half. We never noticed any falling off in performance thereafter, but it did not make the mood of the conductor friendlier to us.

As we came together to rehearse, we would be greeted with "This could be short," or "It's your own time you are wasting," or "Let's get this over, and we'll go home early."

I cannot recall one rehearsal of my many years in the Pops orchestra that finished more than perhaps two minutes before our usual time. I even clearly remember one year when we had reached our final Pops rehearsal with nothing to rehearse. No matter. Handel's *Largo* and Schubert's *Ave Maria* were trotted out, and we spent our entire time rehearsing those two well-known works, pieces which we had so often played through every season, almost without rehearsal! But Arthur got his pound of flesh.

Arthur had another disconcerting little habit. If there were other conductors waiting to conduct us in rehearsal, he would hold us on the stage until about ten minutes before our rehearsal should end. The other conductors simply had to sit in the balcony waiting their turns.

With Arthur's departure, one after another would be brought forward and given their due, usually in such small amounts that enough rehearsal was impossible for these poor souls. Arthur would often stand in the doorway watching one or another with a smile. In most cases, he could have finished rehearsing his own work in time to allow these others to feel comfortable with us. This habit made for overtime, which most of us despised, but it did give Arthur his full amount of rehearsal time.

He could be the most charming person at times, but he could also be very bearish in his attitudes, depending on the moment, what was to be gained from it, or how the music had just been played. We really never knew how to expect him to act but took the moments as they came.

Arthur's baton technique is sufficient for the work he wishes to do. At one moment, having trouble getting from the orchestra the result he wished, he shouted, "What is the trouble with you, people?" The answer came back from the bass section: "You're always ahead of the beat!" As a matter of fact, Arthur's beat is such that this could be literally true. But musicians learn to work with a conductor and can make right come from wrong when it is necessary.

Arthur is indeed a thorough musician with many abilities. He has a genius for knowing what the audience will want to hear, and yet he does not stoop as low as he might in acceding to their wishes. However, there are moments when one might suppose that he has, with the inclusion of some group at the moment enjoying great popular success. But the pieces the Pops orchestra performs with these groups are specially arranged and cannot be played elsewhere. They are well-done, which takes considerable of the sting out of them. And, of course, the old consideration of income must not be forgotten or lost sight of. A good amount of the deficit of the Boston Symphony each year is wiped away by the income from Pops concerts or from Pops recordings.

Certainly, after the fiasco that had occurred during Casella's incumbency, Fiedler's coming into the Pops picture was the best thing that could have happened. He found the answers to the situation then in evidence and has had an astonishing success since he took over.

Guest Conductors

Adrian Boult. Here was one of England's finest conductors. In appearance, a very tall man, whose bristly moustache was one of his identifying features. Unquestionably, he had an authority that communicated itself to all of us. His way with the classics was a beautiful one. Finely educated, his conceptions were on a high scale, no cheapness intruding itself into anything he did with us.

His baton technique was entirely adequate, no unneeded gestures being introduced for the sake of showmanship. We played with him several times, the last instance occurring in Tanglewood, when he had become a much older man. In each instance, we were impressed by his knowledge, his humility, and his earnest attempt to produce the finest music of which we were all capable.

Colin Davis. Colin Davis, an Englishman noted for his conducting works that featured choruses or individual voice soloists, exhibited a love of the music of Sibelius. One after another, he used the Sibelius symphonies as main parts of his programs. Good as they were, they did not erase the memories of those works done by Koussevitzky. The cold winds did not blow for me. But Davis's concept of the choral works he used was of a high order, as was his selection of soloists featured in these works. Janet Baker stood out, as does Jessye Norman. Unquestionably a conductor of merit, he was still a young man in the earlier years of his career.

John Barbirolli. John Barbirolli's reputation had preceded him. He was already known as a very fine conductor, especially in the accompaniment area. We had heard of his cruel treatment by the New York Philharmonic during the years when he was at their head. He had our sympathy in advance.

Playing under him was a real treat. Here was a man, quiet in manner, fully capable of his job, who inspired us to some of our best playing. It was difficult to understand his troubles in New York, except to put it down to his succeeding Toscanini. He had none of the tempestuous qualities that his predecessor had exhibited. By contrast, he must have seemed like a very soft character indeed, one who could be pushed about. That the players proceeded to do, according to all accounts we had heard. The occasions when he conducted us were on his American visits, during which he would fill one or another guest conducting engagements.

He had been a cellist of some accomplishment. He would, when he felt that he could show us exactly what he meant, take a cello in hand and proceed to demonstrate. Through this, he not only showed his own ability as a player, he became one of us. It was obvious that his own efforts were directed to the result of making our own playing more in accord with what he wished. I had never played the Brahms Second Symphony with anyone else in the manner of Barbirolli. He left a lasting impression.

Michael Tilson Thomas. We first saw Tilson Thomas in Tanglewood, if memory does not fail me. He was hailed as a sort of genius, one who had gone through a certain apprenticeship while organizing and directing concerts for Heifetz and Piatigorsky. He followed us to Boston and there became very active with our orchestra. He had a certain ability to conduct the avant-garde works that were coming from our newer composers, and no meter changes seemed to be too great for him to assimilate. He was certainly a man of great talent.

In his attempts to introduce music that our Boston audience had never heard, he sought for works that had been neglected through the years. He found such things as a work by Mozart, which required four groups of players placed at different locations in Symphony Hall. Probably the worst of these "discoveries" was a hexahemeron for six pianos that Liszt had composed some years before. It had never been performed before. Good reason!

Turning to standard repertoire, he exhibited no particular affinity for the works he programmed. Of course, he knew what he was playing, but the extra something that must be introduced into any of the great masterworks seemed to be beyond him.

He had begun at the wrong end of his career. While he should have been learning elsewhere, he had come to us, one of the leading orchestras of this country, if not of the world. He had no place to go but down. As his programs began to pall on our audiences, his strength was not sufficient to allow him to continue on his avant-garde way. He was never more than a frequent guest conductor. He left us very quietly.

Richard Burgin. In addition to his fine qualities as a concertmaster, Richard Burgin exhibited certain talents that made him a perfect candidate for guest conducting. Completely conversant with any score he might conduct, he was never at a loss to bring off a good performance. At any time when Koussevitzky had become too ill to conduct, Burgin could step in and assume the reins and conduct with authority. His beat was a bit heavy, the use of his shoulders too great, which kept any lightness called for by the music from appearing.

In spite of the fact that he had played certain Russian music thorough all the years of Koussevitzky, none of that heritage showed through in his conducting of the same works. He was Russian himself but evidently did not fully agree with the interpretations of his master.

His absentmindedness was proverbial. He could forget his violin and let it ride the streetcar after he had gotten off at his stop, bringing on more than a few panicky moments until he had regained either his Landolfus or G. B. Guadagnini, whichever he happened to be using.

On one occasion, he left his violin on a train in Poland, and much tribulation was his until it was miraculously recovered. The story is told of his parking his car near Symphony Hall, riding the streetcar back to his Jamaica Plain home, finding the garage empty, and reporting his car stolen. Of course, it was discovered just where he had left it.

On one occasion, he left Boston early; took a train to Concord, New Hampshire; and presented himself at the home of a lady who was sponsoring a concert by him. She greeted him with "Why, Mr. Burgin, what a nice surprise. What brings you here?" He then learned that he had the right date but was just a month too early.

Another time, again in a distant town, as he took up his violin to play a recital, he discovered that he had no bow. He had left it in Symphony Hall in the flurry of his sudden departure. Remembering that he had a former pupil who resided in this very town, he made a last-minute call and procured from her a bow, which allowed him to proceed with his program.

With the pianist Leon Vartanian, he gave recitals during which both played from memory. Coming out on stage, they discovered that they had no printed program and so could not know how to start. A borrowed program from someone in the audience allowed them to play the recital as it had been planned.

Burgin, however, did not allow this absentmindedness to interfere with his conducting. He held religiously to the score.

Assessment

If I were asked to grade the conductors under whom I have played during my years with the Boston Symphony, or for whom I have enjoyed working, I should have a little difficulty in answering the question.

I should have to answer that Serge Koussevitzky was easily the most exciting conductor of them all. He had qualities I have not seen in any other man who stood in that position. His dedication was very probably his most outstanding quality, one that led him to work as he did with us. Demanding in his wishes, he was unsatisfied with less than our best, and his own, by the way. He got results that were never attained by any other conductor I could name. Accusations of being cruel and heartless in his treatment of his players must be equated with the results he achieved during his reign.

The list of great masterpieces we played, either old or new, comes to a formidable total and far outweighs any other aspect of his accomplishments. The magnetism exuded by this man communicated itself to his players to a stronger degree than we ever felt from any other conductor. We simply played better than we could.

With Munch, we never knew just where we stood. A man of great stature and high musicianship, his inherent laziness kept him from being a conductor unequaled. In concert, we never knew what to expect. One night we would play a program of extraordinary beauty and excitement. The same program the next night would lack that extra something of the night before. Yet we loved him another way and were sorry to see him go.

But if I were asked to name the best conductor under whom I have played in the Boston Symphony, I should have to name Pierre Monteux. Although he no longer held the position of permanent conductor, his appearances with us were very frequent and gave us plenty of opportunity to know his work, to compare him with others who stood before us.

With no special attribute, he was the most well-rounded conductor, if one considers all aspects of his art. His authority was unquestioned, his ear extraordinary. His baton technique was completely the finest I could name, and over it all the warmth of spirit elicited from us the best of efforts that could be gotten. We played with great enthusiasm, at ease with the conductor, with the music, and the knowledge that we were in the hands of a great master.

Leinsdorf was accurate and cold. We never seemed to warm up to him or to know exactly what he was driving at. We grew bored with the continual Teutonic repertoire to which he seemed addicted and longed for changes in that area of our work. Still, he was an excellent musician and a very good conductor.

With Steinberg, we had already reached the bottom of our performing before he conducted a note. The poor man could not have accomplished his aim of returning us to the sound of Koussevitzky. He had not the faintest inkling of what it had been or how it was gotten. His loyalty to his other orchestra denied the possibility of really working with us toward improving our playing. Another fine musician and an excellent conductor, who had no right to stand before us!

In those early years, I formed the opinion that an orchestra should sound as we did and took it quite for granted. When we had lost Koussevitzky, who insisted on our sound, the vacancy was very apparent, and I longed for its return. But it was never to be.

After Koussevitzky's departure and several years had elapsed, I was astonished to hear a radio interview with one of the players who had certainly been not less than his most dedicated enemy. This player delivered himself of the opinion that there had been none other than Koussevitzky. No one had made the orchestra sound as he had, and no compositions sounded the same as when he had conducted them.

I was later to hear this player speak in the same vein when surrounded by his old colleagues, and to be joined by others who had lived through some of these same years and experiences. In every case, the other speaker had been a key player in the orchestra of Koussevitzky's day and one given to derogatory remarks during the Koussevitzky years. What time does.

Edwards Brothers, Inc.
Thorofare, NJ USA
February 27, 2012